YORK NO

General Editors: Profe
of Stirling) & Professo
University of Beirut)

BEOWULF

Notes by Graham D. Caie

MA (ABERDEEN) PH D (McMASTER)
Senior Lecturer, Department of English,
University of Copenhagen

LONGMAN
YORK PRESS

The author wishes to thank Michael Alexander for permission to quote from his *Beowulf* translation.

YORK PRESS
Immeuble Esseily, Place Riad Solh, Beirut.

LONGMAN GROUP LIMITED
Longman House,
Burnt Mill,
Harlow,
Essex

First published 1984
ISBN 0 582 79252 5
Printed in Hong Kong by
Wilture Printing Co Ltd.

Contents

FAMILY TREES

The Danes (called Ring-Danes, Spear-Danes, Friends of Ing, Scyldings, War-Scyldings)

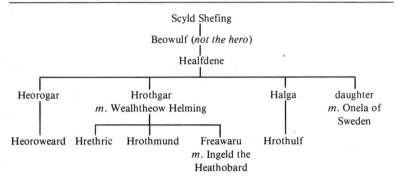

Scyld Shefing
|
Beowulf (*not the hero*)
|
Healfdene

- Heorogar
  - Heoroweard
- Hrothgar *m*. Wealhtheow Helming
  - Hrethric
  - Hrothmund
  - Freawaru *m*. Ingeld the Heathobard
- Halga
  - Hrothulf
- daughter *m*. Onela of Sweden

The Geats (called Weather-Geats, War-Geats, Sea-Geats)

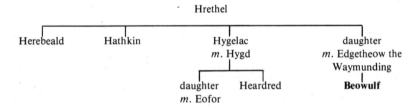

Hrethel

- Herebeald
- Hathkin
- Hygelac *m*. Hygd
  - daughter *m*. Eofor
  - Heardred
- daughter *m*. Edgetheow the Waymunding
  - **Beowulf**

The Swedes (called Scylfings, Battle- or War-Scylfings)

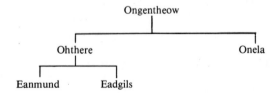

Ongentheow

- Ohthere
  - Eanmund
  - Eadgils
- Onela

Half-Danes (of the Finn Episode)

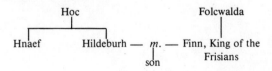

- Hoc
  - Hnaef
  - Hildeburh — *m*. — Finn, King of the Frisians
    - son
- Folcwalda

Part 1

Introduction

Beowulf is one of the greatest epics apart from being the first extended poem in the English language. It describes events that occurred almost fifteen hundred years ago and yet is increasingly popular today amongst students and general public alike, thanks to excellent modern translations. Part of its attraction is due to its being a treasure-house of invaluable information about the culture and customs of early medieval people: it is not to be trusted as a historical work, but through it we come to know about Germanic attitudes to fate, revenge, the supernatural, poetry and worldly goods. In it we learn about woman's role as peace-weaver, funeral customs, art, weapons, the heroic code and much more. It illuminates that fascinating twilight period when pagan heroic and early Christian concepts, ideals and cultures were inextricably interwoven, and it gives us a glimpse of the hopes and fears of tribes living under the constant threat of war or natural disaster. It is a story of one man's heroic fight to bring lasting peace, order and harmony to a society living under such a threat, which in this poem is the unwarranted attack of malignant monsters.

The message of *Beowulf* is clear: in spite of the apparently impossible odds that life presents us with, one must not surrender but courageously fight until death. It is a message that appears both pessimistic, for Beowulf's peaceful reign does end tragically, and optimistic, because of this example of outstanding determination. By creating this mixed mood of sadness and joy the poet expresses some basic paradoxes of life that modern readers understand only too well. He questions man's relationship to fate; how do we treat success, riches and prosperity when we know they are passing? How do we face tragedy and death when the afterlife is so uncertain (for the poet withholds the Christian solution)? How do we fight despair and live with hope? One critic sums up the message as how to live a life that ends with death. But it is not only a philosophical work. It is a tale of adventure, the supernatural, battles and heroes that is as gripping as any modern superman story.

The manuscript

Beowulf survives in one manuscript preserved in the British Library, London. The 'Beowulf Manuscript' (officially called MS. BL. Cotton

Vitellius A. XV) measures 23×15cm and the pages are of vellum (calf skin). In addition to a number of prose works the manuscript contains the poem *Judith*, and the governing principle behind the selection of material appears to be the theme of monsters. We can be certain that the manuscript was written around the year 1000 and that two scribes copied it. The writing is clear and the dialect that of late West Saxon, classical Old English, although we can see traces of Anglian dialect from an earlier version. Both the author and scribes are unknown and the title *Beowulf* was first used in the nineteenth century. The poetry is written out as prose, as was usual because of the value of vellum, and there are many abbreviations (for the same reason) in the twenty-line pages. There is little punctuation and compound words are not joined, so modern editors have certain problems.

Problems are increased by the fact that the manuscript was damaged in a fire in 1731 when many medieval manuscripts in the collection of Sir Robert Cotton (1571–1631) were burned. Many pages were scorched round the edges and have since crumbled away, making letters and words illegible. In 1787 Thorkelin, an Icelander in the service of the Danish government, made two copies of the poem at a time when more letters were legible. These invaluable documents are preserved in The Royal Library, Copenhagen.

Other Old English manuscripts

We have only about thirty thousand lines of Old English (or Anglo-Saxon) poetry extant, so the 3182 lines of *Beowulf* constitute a vital part of the corpus. We can guess, however, that this was only a fraction of the Old English verse written down, while even more would have circulated orally. Four major manuscripts with poetry survive, all written in the classical West Saxon dialect of about the year 1000: The Exeter Book in the Chapter Library of Exeter Cathedral, the Junius XI Manuscript in the Bodleian Library, Oxford, the Vercelli Manuscript in the Cathedral Library, Vercelli, Italy, and the British Library *Beowulf* Manuscript. Much of the verse is religious, for example biblical narratives of *Genesis, Exodus* and *Daniel* and some saints' lives— *Juliana, Guthlac, Elene*; and there are historical poems such as *The Battle of Maldon*, riddles and maxims, not to mention the beautiful lyrics of The Exeter Book, such as *The Wanderer, The Seafarer, The Wife's Lament, The Husband's Message* and *The Ruin*. The early Old English poem *Widsith* with its lists of legendary heroes, many of whom are found in *Beowulf*, bears witness to the fact that there must have been much poetry in the Germanic tradition and that Ingeld, Eormanric and Offa would have been well known to the Anglo-Saxon audience. This explains why we are not told the complete tale, for example, of Ingeld; we are expected to know it, for the poet uses it to elicit a specific mood.

The date and location of *Beowulf*

Although we can determine the date of the manuscript and the dialect of the scribe, there is much debate about the date of the composition of the poem itself. It is traditionally thought to have been composed early in the eighth century in the Anglian dialect, but recently scholars have pushed the date as far forward as possible into the tenth century. The confusion arises from the nature of the composition of the poem. Was it first composed and written in its entirety as we know it today, or did it gradually grow as it was passed on by word of mouth in an oral tradition? Few would dispute the fact that there were oral tales about parts of the *Beowulf* poem—for example, the story of Ingeld and Finn, and Hygelac's fatal expedition. Linguistic evidence shows an earlier Anglian source and some archaisms seem to place the poem squarely in the eighth century (the second scribe of the *Beowulf* manuscript is less consistent than the first in changing Anglian forms to the West Saxon dialect). Others claim that the sophistication of Christian allusions— for example, the term *non* (l. 1600) for the Church Office of None, and the references to Cain and Creation—points to a later date. There are also arguments for and against the fact that the Viking invasions beginning in the late eighth century would have made a complimentary tale about Danes unlikely if written later than that date. Consolation can be found in the fact that scholars cannot agree on the date, as the most recent book on the dating of *Beowulf* shows. It would have been helpful to students to say that the poem is about events in the sixth century, was composed in the eighth and written down in the (late) tenth.

We do have some pointers as to the date of the events that take place in the story. King Hygelac did exist as Chlochilaichus or Huiglaucus/ Hugletus, who, according to Gregory of Tours (died 594) in his *History of the Franks*, was killed in battle *c.*520 (see ll. 1202 ff., 2354 ff., 2501 ff. and 2910 ff.). The wars with the Swedes occurred in the 530s, so we can fix a date of early sixth century for the events in the poem. This would of course place the story firmly in pre-Christian Scandinavia.

The poem has nothing to do with England or the Anglo-Saxons, except in spirit, although the author has an English audience. It could be compared with Chaucer's *Troilus and Criseyde*, which is set in Troy but intended for an English audience. The location of *Beowulf* is Scandinavia, initially Zealand in Denmark. Hrothgar is the legendary king of Denmark, Ro, who held his court at Lethra and founded the town of Roskilde ('Ro's fountain'; the cathedral of Roskilde is still the burial place of Danish monarchs). Lethra is said to be modern Lejre, situated·

near Roskilde and strategically important at the head of Roskilde fjord. The second part of the poem takes place in Geatland which is thought to be in southern Sweden, possibly inland from Gothenburg; and their enemies, called the Swedes, would have lived just north of them. But in this poem neither locations nor historical events matter. The distant Scandinavian setting would be far enough away for dragons and monsters and yet the human actors would have been closely related to the Anglo-Saxons in many respects.

The Anglo-Saxons and their language

Old English is generally the term used for the language of the Anglo-Saxons and covers the period from the Germanic settlements in the fifth century until just after the Norman Conquest (1066) when French influence radically changed the English language.

On the fall of the Roman Empire the Roman military forces were recalled from Britain in the late fourth and early fifth centuries, leaving the native Celtic tribes, along with those Romans who had settled in Britain, to tackle increasingly strong attacks from Germanic tribes on the continent. Among early invaders were the Jutes with Hengest and Horsa as their leaders, perhaps the same Hengest mentioned in the Finn Episode in *Beowulf*. By the early sixth century the invasions were more successful and the invaders settled. It was about this time that a British leader called Arthur opposed the Saxons and the brief historical mentions of his exploits were to mushroom into the myth of King Arthur, although it is unlikely that he was a monarch.

By the sixth century we can talk about Anglo-Saxon England, for the Celtic tribes were now driven to the extremities of Britain and over to Britanny in northern France by the Jutes, Angles and Saxons. Christianity also came to Britain at this time. Pope Gregory sent Augustine to England in 597, and with such an enlightened and diplomatic missionary the Roman Catholic church quickly spread, although there were many cases of lapses into heathen practices which Bede (?673–735) describes in his *Ecclesiastical History of the English People* (731). The Roman church grew in strength because of its well-organised administrative machinery and finally ousted the monastic and more ascetic Celtic church which had its English centre at Lindisfarne in Northumbria. The authority of Rome was established after the Synod of Whitby in 664.

Gradually England became united with a strong Wessex monarchy. Both unity and Christianity were seriously threatened by the Viking raids of the ninth century. This was the time of King Alfred of Wessex (849–99) who proved to be a man of both learning and military skill. He made a treaty with Guthrum the Dane in 886 and ruled all England south of the Humber. Alfred complained in the Preface to his translation of Gregory's *Pastoral Care* about the poverty of learning in England: 'There were few who could understand their services in English, or even translate a letter from Latin into English.' Alfred translated much from Latin into Old English, including Boethius's *Consolation of Philosophy* and works by St Augustine; he inspired the compilation of the *Anglo-Saxon Chronicle* and established a legal code. Danish influence continued in the eastern part of England—East Anglia, Northumbria and the North-east Midlands—but peace was achieved between Alfred and the Danes.

The languages of Angles, Saxons and Jutes were descended from a common Germanic source. Gradually a common Anglo-Saxon language emerged with strong dialects, depending on the geographical area. Northumbria, Mercia and East Anglia (northern and eastern areas) had been settled by the Angles and this dialect is called Anglian; the Jutes had taken Kent (Kentish dialect) and the Saxons the area of Essex, Wessex and Sussex (West Saxon dialect). Most of the surviving Old English poetry we have is written in a late Old English (*c*.1000) West Saxon dialect.

A note on the text

These notes are intended for readers of *Beowulf* in the original Old English as well as in modern English translations. The Old English edition chosen here is that of F. Klaeber, *Beowulf and the Fight at Finnsburg*, D.C. Heath and Company, Boston, 3rd edition, 1950, and the translation is that of Michael Alexander, *Beowulf: A Verse Translation*, Penguin Books, Harmondsworth, 1973.

Line-numbering refers to the Klaeber edition and should help those working with a different translation.

Michael Alexander's work is an original, poetic rendition of the text and not a literal translation. Consequently the modern English in brackets in the Notes and Glossary sections must not be taken as necessarily a direct translation of the Old English quoted. Sometimes the literal translation of the Old English is added to convey a precise meaning.

These Notes do not comment on linguistic or editorial complexities in the Old English text, but concentrate on ideas, background information and other explanatory material which aid an appreciation of the poem.

Part 2

Summaries
of BEOWULF

A general summary

The poet begins with the mythic history of the Danes, concentrating on the story of the illustrious ruler Scyld Shefing, founder of the Scyld dynasty. As a child he had mysteriously arrived, alone, by boat; he had ruled triumphantly and on his death his body was returned to the sea. We sense the ebb and flow of one reign after the other until we reach the kingship of Hrothgar, whose glorious and peaceful reign is symbolised by his creation of the great hall Heorot. The harmony of the hall—and thus of Denmark—is broken by the nightly attacks of the monster Grendel who kills thirty men on his first visit. The reign of terror continues for twelve years, by which time Hrothgar and his country are in despair and some turn to heathen practices.

Beowulf, the nephew of King Hygelac of the Geats, after hearing of Grendel's tyranny, sets sail for Denmark with fourteen followers and is immediately recognised as a hero who can save the Danes. Beowulf presents himself to Hrothgar, outlines his lineage and vows to cleanse Heorot by killing Grendel barehanded. Beowulf is very well received, but at a banquet Unferth, one of Hrothgar's counsellors, doubts Beowulf's prowess, accusing him of losing a swimming match with Breca. This slur on his character gives Beowulf a chance to describe his victory and strength in an underwater battle with sea monsters, thus foreshadowing his later triumphs.

That night Grendel attacks Heorot and kills Handscio before Beowulf grasps one of the monster's arms in a deadly clinch. Grendel realises that he has met his match, but can only escape by losing his arm. Mortally wounded he returns to his lair. There is great rejoicing at Heorot the next day and Beowulf is acclaimed a great hero, comparable to the dragon-slayer Sigemund and unlike the niggardly King Heremod. Beowulf receives much treasure in reward from Hrothgar who symbolically adopts him as a son. At the height of the rejoicing the sad tale of Finn is narrated, thus stressing the fragility and brevity of peace and joy. Hrothgar's wife, Wealhtheow, asks Beowulf to aid her sons in the future.

That night Grendel's mother attacks Heorot, kills Ashhere, Hrothgar's counsellor, and retrieves her son's severed arm. Beowulf is not present but the next day he prepares to attack Grendel's mother in her underwater lair. The hell-like location and frightening surroundings are described in graphic detail. The fight in the subterranean cave is fierce, both sides evenly matched in strength, until Beowulf sees a giant sword on the cave wall which he uses to kill the monster and to cut off Grendel's head, after which the sword-blade melts. Beowulf returns triumphant with the sword-hilt and Grendel's head. In the midst of great rejoicing at the hero's return Hrothgar delivers a long discourse about the dangers of pride, the mutability of the world and about his own prosperity and trouble. After exchanging gifts, farewell speeches and promises of loyalty, Beowulf and his men return to their homeland with a ship laden with armour and gifts.

When they arrive at the land of the Geats the treasure is taken to King Hygelac's hall. Mention of the young and wise Hygd, Hygelac's wife, leads the poet to a comparison between her and the proud and cruel Thryth. Beowulf tells Hygelac of his adventures and, at the mention of Hrothgar's daughter Freawaru, interweaves the story of her and Ingeld. Beowulf predicts that the intended marriage between the Danish princess and the Heathobard prince will not end the feud between these two tribes but will cause fresh disaster. Beowulf then liberally disperses the gifts he received from Hrothgar to Hygelac and Hygd and in return receives treasure from them.

In the second part of the epic the poet jumps ahead to the time when Beowulf has ruled for fifty years after the deaths of Hygelac and his son Heardred. Tragedy strikes again, this time in the shape of a dragon which ravages Beowulf's realm. The dragon has guarded treasure until a fugitive slave robbed the hoard in order to gain favour with his lord. This had enraged the dragon which took violent revenge on the country and burned Beowulf's hall. Beowulf decides to fight the dragon single-handed and has a fireproof iron shield made. The poet praises Beowulf's bravery which is as great as when he was a youth, and he recalls events that occurred earlier in Beowulf's life: the battles after his return to Geatland, the death of Hygelac, Beowulf's refusal of the throne and generous offer to aid Heardred, Heardred's death at the hands of the Swedes and how Beowulf avenged his death. The poet then returns to Beowulf's preparations for his battle with the dragon. He reconnoitres the place of the dragon's lair with companions to whom he delivers a farewell speech which is followed by a résumé of the history of the Geatish royal house, in particular the encounters with the Swedes. Beowulf then enters the dragon's cave, draws his sword and encounters the fiery dragon. His sword fails him and he is overwhelmed by fire. All his companions retreat into the woods, except Wiglaf who comes to his rescue. The lineage of Wiglaf is described, as well as the history of his sword. Wiglaf rebukes the cowardly companions. In the battle Beowulf's sword, Nailing, snaps, but Wiglaf deals a decisive blow which

Beowulf follows up with a knife wound, but is fatally wounded. Wiglaf tends the dying Beowulf and brings the treasure out of the cave at Beowulf's request. Beowulf gives thanks for having won the treasure and requests a burial mound to be build for him, Beowulf's barrow, on a headland as a memorial. He gives his armour to Wiglaf before he dies.

Wiglaf reproaches the others for cowardice, and while he guards the body of his lord, he sends a messenger to Beowulf's people with the sad news. The messenger recalls past wars with the Franks and Swedes and predicts future attacks now they are lordless. Wiglaf orders the treasure to be taken from the dragon's cave, the dragon to be pushed into the sea and a funeral pyre to be built. Beowulf is placed on the pyre along with his armour; then the flames rise and the people lament the loss of this great hero. A burial mound is erected on the remains of the pyre and the treasure from the dragon's hoard placed in it. Finally twelve noble warriors ride round the barrow praising and mourning for Beowulf.

Detailed summaries

The history of the Danish kings   lines 1–63

The poem opens with an account of the mythical founder of the Scylding dynasty, the foundling Scyld Shefing. He became a glorious king, conquering all neighbouring lands, and his son, Beow, succeeded him with equal success. The poet moralises about the need for a young prince to be liberal with gifts, so that in later years old friends will serve and support him. Scyld's funeral is described: at his own request his body was placed in a ship laden with treasure and armour in the same manner in which he had mysteriously arrived in Denmark, and the boat is launched, heading for its unknown destination. Healfdene followed Beow as king of the Danes and one of his four children was the famous Hrothgar.

NOTES AND GLOSSARY:
In this opening passage we sense the passing of time, the brevity of a king's reign, however glorious, and the cyclical pattern of one chief succeeded by another. This pattern is strengthened by the story of Scyld's mysterious arrival and departure to the unknown from whence he came.

Hwaet (Attend):   (1.1) it is normally accepted that this common opening in heroic poetry is the Anglo-Saxon poet's call for order and silence

aethelingas (athelings): (1.3) princes or heroes

Scyld Scefing (Shefing): (1.4) according to myth the founder of the Danish Scylding royal house. *Scyld* means 'shield' and *Scefing* might imply 'sheaf', thereby having fertility connotations. He is the mysterious saviour figure akin to King Arthur, whose departure resembles that of Scyld

meodosetla (mead-benches): (1.5) mead is a drink of honey and water fermented. The warriors' mead-bench stands for the hall itself which in turn symbolises the independent power of the ruler

hronrade (whale-road): (1.10) a metaphor or kenning (see p.82) for the sea

Liffrea/wuldres Wealdend (Life-bestowing Wielder of Glory): (1.16) God is often described in terms that highlight one of his specific functions: here the Lord of life gives an heir

Beowulf (Beow): (1.18) the son of Scyld, not the poem's hero

fromum feohgiftum (give a free hand): (1.21) this is the first of many interspersed moralising comments. It stresses the need to be generous in order to ensure later allies

lofdaedum (by glorious action): (1.24) literally 'with deeds causing praise'. The final aim of the Germanic warrior is to build as great a reputation as a hero as possible

beaga bryttan (dealer of wound gold): (1.35) a common epithet for 'lord'. Gold was kept in the form of arm-bands or collars

madma fela (A mound of treasures): (1.36) ship burials such as that of Scyld were common in the pre-Christian north, for example the Sutton Hoo find in East Anglia and in late Viking times in Scandinavia. Swords, armour and costly jewelry would constitute the treasure

aet frumsceafte (at the outset): (1.45) this refers to the time when Scyld arrived in Denmark as a child

segen (*signum*): (1.47) a standard or sceptre, emblem of kingship. A sceptre was also found in the Sutton Hoo find

Healfdene: (1.57) son of Beow, father of Hrothgar

Onela: (1.62) a Swedish king

The building of Heorot   lines 64–85

King Hrothgar became a famous ruler and had a great hall built, called Heorot, larger than all others on earth. He kept his word and generously bestowed treasure. The time had not yet come when Heorot was to be burned down and blood feud would break out.

NOTES AND GLOSSARY:
The hall symbolises the great prosperity and fame of Hrothgar and the Danes. The poet frequently hints at future disaster at points of celebration, thus stressing the fragility of worldly joy.

medoaern (mead-hall): (l.69) the central place in the heroic society where the king rules and warriors meet and drink mead
middangeard (middle earth): (l.75) this implies a view of the world as the centre between heaven and hell
Heort (*Heorot*): (l.78) the name suggests 'hart', a royal symbol. Possibly the hall had horn-shaped gables
beagas daelde (gave out rings): (l.80) the king was often called a 'ring-giver', as it was part of his function to distribute treasure, often gold in the form of arm-bands
heathowylma (torch flame): (l.82) literally, 'hostile flames'. This is a reference to the Heathobard conflict. There is no mention of Heorot being burned down in *Beowulf*, but the story would have been popular
athumsweoran (in sworn kindred): (l.84) this is an allusion to the Heathobard incident. Hrothgar's daughter Freawaru is to marry the Heathobard Ingeld and Beowulf later (ll.2024–69) predicts a feud between the tribes. This minor 'digression' foreboding disaster at a time of peace serves as a link between the Heorot and the Grendel passages—from human to demonic treachery

***

Grendel is described   lines 86–114

***

Grendel hears the joy and the song of Creation coming from the hall and is enraged. He is described as a demonic enemy, of Cain's descent, who lives as an outcast in the moors and fens.

NOTES AND GLOSSARY:
ellengaest (powerful spirit): (l.86) Grendel
sang scopes (song of the poet): (l.90) the poet played an important function in society and was called 'scop', creator
wlitebeorhtne wang (a plain bright to look on): (l.93) the poet sings of the Creation of the world and the plain is Eden. It is fitting that the description of Hrothgar's creation of a harmonious hall and country is followed by this account of a Paradise before evil attacked. There is continual contrast between the light and brightness of order and cosmos and the darkness of evil and chaos. Heorot and Grendel's lair are

diametrically opposed to each other, hence
Grendel's inherent hatred

feond on helle (enemy from hell): (l.101) Grendel is described in terms
of the devil

mearcstapa (the march is his haunt): (l.103) 'march' means the bound-
aries of the country and this name implies his state
of exile from civilisation

Caines cynne (kindred of Cain): (l.107) Cain, the evil son of Adam who
killed his brother Abel (see the Bible, Genesis 4:8),
came to represent the source of all unrepented evil
in the world

eotenas (giants): (l.112) see the Bible, Genesis 6:4. All kinds of
supernatural beings—monsters, ogres and elves—
are considered demonic

Grendel attacks lines 115–163

Grendel's first attack is described. He strikes at night, carrying off
thirty warriors tò his lair. There is great mourning in Heorot the next
day and Hrothgar grieves for the loss. The attacks continue for twelve
years and Grendel now 'rules' Heorot which stands empty.

NOTES AND GLOSSARY:

Hring-Dene (Ring-Danes): (l.116) another term for the Danes; 'ring'
refers to the armour made out of rings

on raeste (on their pallets): (l.122) while in bed

healthegnes hete (hall-thane's hatred): (l.142) a thane is a retainer and
Grendel is described with understatement as a new
resident in Heorot

twelf wintra tid (twelve long winters): (l.147) a conventional time
implying a long period

wine Scyldinga (the Friend of the Scyldings): (l.148) Hrothgar

beorhtre bote (bright man-price): (l.158) the compensation the murderer would be obliged to pay the family of his vic-
tim. Naturally Grendel feels no such obligation.
Grendel is opposed to all that ordered society
believes in. The mention of compensation, Cain,
thane and so on suggests the partially human
nature of Grendel

deorc deathscua (dark death-shadow): (l.160) Grendel, implying the
devil

helrunan (hell's familiars): (l.163) demons, witches

feond mancynnes (the enemy of man): (l.164) in Old English poetry
this means the devil and here suggests Grendel's
inherent hatred of mankind

The Danes become idolaters   lines 163–193

Hrothgar and his counsellors are in despair and none can suggest a solution. Sometimes they sacrificed to heathen idols and prayed to pagan gods. The poet rebukes them for such practices.

NOTES AND GLOSSARY:

gifstol (treasure throne): (l.168) Hrothgar's throne where he dispensed treasure. Possibly God prevents evil from reaching this central point

gastbona (Slayer of souls): (l.177) a heathen god or devil. The poet wishes to stress by this epithet the impossibility of a heathen god sending help. This passage is much disputed. Either the Danes revert to paganism at times of trouble, as the Anglo-Saxons did, or it means that they were not yet converted (but the many Christian allusions make the latter interpretation difficult). The poet is describing the lowest possible point for Hrothgar and his men when totally without hope

Beowulf's journey and arrival in Denmark   lines 194–228

Beowulf, King Hygelac of Geatland's nephew, a man renowned for his strength, sets out for Denmark. He picks fourteen good thanes and sets sail with his fully armoured men. They arrive in Denmark and give thanks to God for their safe crossing.

NOTES AND GLOSSARY:

The description of Beowulf's voyage is reminiscent of the arrival of Scyld Scefing, another saviour figure.

Higelaces thegn (one of *Hygelac*'s followers): (l.194) Beowulf

ythlidan (wave-cutter): (l.198) a metaphor or kenning for a boat. The tone and style change from the previous passage of despair to a more poetic and colourful language

swanrade (swan's riding): (l.200) a kenning for the sea

sundwudu (sound-wood): (l.208) a kenning for a boat

Wedera leode (Weather-Geats): (l.225) a title for the Geats of Hygelac

The Danish Coastguard challenges Beowulf   lines 229–319

The coastguard watches Beowulf's arrival, rides to the shore and challenges the warriors. He is surprised by the open nature of their arrival. He can immediately see that Beowulf has a heroic look and bearing. He demands to know their names, lineage and reason for coming. Beowulf replies that they are Hygelac's men, he is son of Edgetheow and they come to help Hrothgar in his present distress. The coastguard praises Beowulf and guides him to Heorot after posting men to guard Beowulf's boat until they return.

NOTES AND GLOSSARY:

weard (watchman): (l.229) the coastguard. Beowulf's arrival is described through the eyes of objective observers and thus the poet can stress Beowulf's heroic nature and immediate acceptance

aenlic ansyn (head of a hero): (l.251) literally, 'unique appearance'

leassceaweras (undeclared spies): (l.253) the coastguard simply performs his task of protecting the shores. It would be normal to demand these explanations

se yldesta (The captain): (l.258) literally, 'the eldest', hence 'chief'

wordhord onleac (unlocked his word-hoard): (l.259) simply means 'spoke'. The expression shows the value placed on language by the Anglo-Saxons and the need to use it economically

Ecgtheow (Edgetheow): (l.263) Beowulf's father, who was a Waymunding married to the Geatish princess, sister of Hygelac. Beowulf correctly mentions his king first, then his nation, his father and much later his own name. This is necessary in order to establish oneself as a friend

bot (settlement): (l.281) literally, 'remedy'. Beowulf frequently refers to Grendel's deeds and the state of Heorot in medical terms, as if a disease had gripped the hall

line 296: the coastguard's reply implies that he is confident that Beowulf will be successful and return home safely

Eoforlic scionan (boar-shapes shone out): (l.303) the boar is a royal emblem. This is a disputed passage, but the implication is that the Geats are wearing helmets with boar-shapes on them. Such a helmet has been found in England at Benty Grange, Derbyshire

---

The Geats arrive at Heorot and are met by Wulfgar   lines 320–370

Beowulf and his men disarm and are met by Hrothgar's chamberlain, Wulfgar, who also expresses surprise at their bold arrival. Beowulf gives his name and asks to see Hrothgar. Wulfgar is immediately impressed by Beowulf and begs the king to give the Geats an audience.

NOTES AND GLOSSARY:

lixte se leoma (its radiance lighted): (l.311) Heorot is again seen as the greatest, most beautiful and radiant hall. Both Beowulf and the hall are described in terms of light, gold and splendour

aescholt ufan graeg (an ash-wood grey-tipped): (l.330) a spear with a grey point. As a sign of peace they leave weapons outside Heorot

wlonc haeleth (high-mannered chieftain): (l.331) Wulfgar, Hrothgar's chamberlain, who has to screen all who approach the king

for wlenco . . . for wraecsithum (not exile but adventure): (l.338) literally, 'for pride [daring] nor for exile'. These are the only two reasons Wulfgar can imagine why anyone would leave home

Beowulf: (l.343) this is the first time he mentions his name and it comes modestly after the description of lineage and character

beaga bryttan (giver of arm-bands): (l.352) this epithet stresses Hrothgar's generosity and popularity as a king

---

Hrothgar welcomes Beowulf who offers to slay Grendel lines 371−490

Hrothgar has already heard of Beowulf's great strength and he knew his father Edgetheow. He gives thanks to God for sending him. Wulfgar summons Beowulf who enters dramatically and greets Hrothgar warmly. He immediately states his purpose in coming, namely to defeat Grendel and cleanse Heorot. He makes the heroic boast that he will fight with bare hands, as Grendel will be unarmed. Should he be defeated he would like Hrothgar to send his armour back to Hygelac, but there will be nothing left of his body, if Grendel takes him.

Hrothgar heartily thanks Beowulf and reminds him of the help he gave Edgetheow when he sought refuge in Denmark: Hrothgar paid reparation on his behalf and Edgetheow swore allegiance to Hrothgar. The king summarises the terror and havoc Grendel has caused and laments the number of men that are dead.

NOTES AND GLOSSARY:

Hrethel Geata: (l.374) Beowulf's maternal grandfather

holdne wine (proven ally): (l.376) we later learn that Edgetheow was indebted to Hrothgar. There is a suggestion here that Hrothgar supposes that Beowulf has come to repay this debt

mundgripe (hand's grasp): (l.380) the legendary strength of Beowulf's grasp, equal to thirty men, is later demonstrated

smithes orthancum (smith's skill): (l.406) refers to Beowulf's armour. The poet is able to stress the honour given to Beowulf by letting him retain his armour

niceras (sea-serpents): (l.422) this is an allusion to the Breca episode which is about to come, and it looks forward also to the underwater fight with Grendel's mother. He begins with a boast, expected of a hero and which cannot be called immodest, and ends by humbly submitting to fate. His battles with giants and sea-monsters already place him amongst the legendary heroes

Heorot faelsian (to cleanse . . . Heorot): (l.432) Beowulf often uses the image of cleansing or healing the Danish state

se aeglaeca (this unlovely one): (l.433) literally, 'ugly one'; 'ugly' had originally associations of evil, for example the Ugly Sisters of pantomime

mid grape (with bare hands): (l.438) Beowulf will meet Grendel on equal terms, yet later we hear that weapons cannot harm the monster. There is a progressive lessening of Beowulf's strength and of the power of his weapons as the fights continue

se the hine death nimeth (He who is chosen): (l.441) there is an implicit belief here in fate or predestination; cf. line 455, 'Fate will take its course'

Weland (Wayland): (l.455) the mythical smith with magical powers who fashioned armour for the great heroes. He is like Vulcan in Greek myth

Wyrd (Weird): (ll.455, 472) Fate (compare the 'weird sisters' in Shakespeare's *Macbeth*). Weird implies the amoral forces of the world—neither evil nor benevolent—that rule all things without any cause and effect, such as weather, disease, or accidents. In Christian terms the word came to signify Divine Providence

Heatholafe: (l.460) Beowulf's father Edgetheow defeated Heatholaf of the Wylfing tribe, but the Geats were unable to pay the necessary compensation. He was given protection by the young Hrothgar who paid Heatholaf's 'man-price'. Edgetheow could then return to the Geats, but naturally he pledged future support to Hrothgar. This episode shows the function of 'ring-giving': it is an attempt to ensure future support in case of hard times

Heregar (Heorogar): (l.467) Hrothgar's elder brother

hyntho (humiliation): (l.475) Hrothgar makes a clear distinction between the fame, richness and power of the Danes in
his earlier reign and the present state of humiliation and depression

---

Unferth challenges Beowulf   lines 491—606

There are great celebrations amongst Danes and Geats at Heorot which
once more echoes with the sound of laughter and song. A note of discord is introduced by Unferth who questions Beowulf's prowess,
accusing him of being unable to keep his boast in the Breca swimming
match. He also doubts that Beowulf can conquer Grendel. This taunt
gives Beowulf a chance to tell about his successes and strength without
being immodest. He not only won the match after five days' swimming, but fought sea monsters while fully armed, thereby clearing the
sea of dangers. Beowulf then questions Unferth's prowess and there
has been no sign of him attacking Grendel to protect his lord.

NOTES AND GLOSSARY:
Unferth: (l.499) the name implies 'lack of peace' and he lives
up to this as he disrupts the celebrations and casts
doubt on Beowulf's fame
for wlence (for pride): (l.508) pride was the major sin in early medieval
society. A hero had to show great courage but not
overstep his function or be haughty. Unferth's
accusation is one of excess in self-confidence
dolgilpe (trite boast): (l.509) the hero was expected to make a formal
boast before an enterprise, as Beowulf later does
before the Grendel mission. It is a flaw, however,
to break this earnest oath or to make it for frivolous reasons. Unferth suggests that this contest was
one of self-indulgence. Beowulf amply demonstrates, however, that the adventure had widespreading consequences, for example, keeping the
seas free from monsters
garsecg (Spear-Man): (l.515) the sea (Neptune?)
Heatho-Raemes (Battle-Reams): (l.519) a south Norwegian tribe
sunu Beanstanes (the son of Beanstan): (l.524) Breca, who was known
in other heroic legends
grim on grape (pinned in his grip): (l.555) we are meant to see a parallel
here with the later scenes of battle
unfaegne eorl (the man undoomed): (l.573) that is, the man not destined to die [is often saved by fate if he is courageous]

under heofones hwealf (under heaven's vault): (l.576) implies that the world is like a hall with the heavens as a vault. This is a common theme in Old English

Finna land (coasts of the Lapps): (l.580) Finland. The exaggerated distance stresses the legendary nature of the feat. It is common for the young hero to demonstrate his prowess in this way

helle: (l.588) Beowulf prophesies that Unferth will go to hell for his fratricide. His sin places him in the same category as Cain

lines 590–601: although Beowulf refers to Unferth's cowardice, there may be hidden criticism of the Danes who have offered Grendel no resistance

nydbade (tribute): (l.598) the image is one of Grendel as overlord or tyrant exacting money—in this case it is men—from his subjects

morgenleoht (breaking light): (l.604) this section is full of imagery of light, sun, dawn, hope, trust and laughter, in contrast to the earlier dark, night and sadness imagery before Beowulf's arrival. In Old English the Danes are here referred to as *Beorht-Dena*, 'Bright-Danes'

Queen Wealhtheow entertains Beowulf and there is great feasting
lines 607–661

NOTES AND GLOSSARY:

Wealhtheow: (l.612) Hrothgar's queen. Her duty is to be a 'weaver of peace' and she is seen here to be fulfilling her function perfectly. She offers the cup in correct order of precedence and ensures that all is peaceful in the hall

ides Helminga (the Helming princess): (l.620) Wealhtheow, referring to her own tribe before marriage

beaghroden cwen (flashing-armed queen): (l.623) a reference to her jewelry and wealth in gold arm-bands

lines 636–8: here Beowulf formally makes his heroic boast or pledge, as is fitting for a hero before his conflict

Naefre...tha (Never...you): (l.655) Hrothgar pays Beowulf the compliment of handing over control of his hall (and hence his power) to another, which he has never done previously. In the circumstances this might be considered a doubtful compliment. Hrothgar also ensures that he leaves Heorot before Grendel pays his visit

Beowulf prepares for battle   lines 662–702

Hrothgar leaves Beowulf as guardian of Heorot. Beowulf disarms, claiming that he will defeat Grendel by force of strength, not by weapons. God will decide who shall win. Beowulf goes to bed and the poet tells us that God was to help Beowulf to be victorious.

NOTES AND GLOSSARY:

Kyningwuldor (the King of Glory): (l.665) the poet implies here that God 'appoints' Beowulf to be Grendel's slayer

Tha . . . hildegeatwe (He . . . war): (l.671) normally one would expect an armouring scene at this point in an epic, but here we have a 'disarming' scene. Beowulf is as yet unaware that Grendel cannot be killed by weapons; he will trust in his own strength and God's favour

thara goda (the art): (l.681) Beowulf claims that Grendel, whose nature he appears to know instinctively, has not the art to wield weapons. Grendel is made a curious mixture of beast and uncultivated, sinful man

wigspeda gewiofu (in the web of fate): (l.697) the image of destiny as a spun web was common. Here the poet implies that within the predestined order God was to aid the Geats. This suggests a benevolent providence. It is also typical of the poet to tell us the outcome before the event and dispel suspense

The fight with Grendel   lines 702–824

Grendel comes stealthily through the night, bent on killing more. He bursts open the hall door and sees the sleeping soldiers, but Beowulf keeps watch from his bed. Grendel snatches a Geat warrior, tears his body and devours it. He then reaches out for Beowulf who is too quick for him as he grips the monster in a deadly clinch. Grendel immediately realises that he has met someone stronger than himself and tries to escape into the darkness, but Beowulf holds on. The poet views the scene from outside Heorot where the listening Danes hear the great noise of fierce combat and the groans of Grendel. Beowulf's men run to his assistance with weapons which prove useless against Grendel whose arm is torn off by Beowulf's grip. The monster escapes to his lair, mortally wounded.

NOTES AND GLOSSARY:

sceadugenga (walker in the night): (l.703) Grendel; again he is described in terms of darkness, night, evil and ignorance

mynte se manscatha (the spoiler meant): (l.712) literally, 'the evil-doer intended [to kill]'. One critic points out the number of 'meant' verbs connected with Grendel. Unlike his adversary, Grendel is thwarted as he lacks insight and wisdom (cf. ll.731 and 762)

Ne waes thaet forma sith (That was not the first visit): (l.716) this is one of the many examples of Old English understatement

Ne waes thaet wyrd tha gen (It was not to be): (l.734) no suspense, only a balance between Grendel's doomed hopes and our knowledge of the outcome

slaependne rinc (a sleeping soldier): (l.741) much later (l.2076) we are told his name—Handscio. It is curious that Beowulf allows one of his men to be killed. Perhaps he is a victim sacrificed so that Beowulf can watch Grendel's tactics

rinc on raeste (warrior . . . at rest): (l.747) Beowulf

he onfeng . . . gesaet (but the faster man . . . arm): (ll.748–9) C.L. Wrenn translates this confusing section: 'Quickly did he [Beowulf] perceive that plan of malice; and he sat right up violently so as to drive back Grendel's arm'

fyrena hyrde (the upholder of evils): (l.750) Grendel; literally, 'the guardian of sins'

Dryhtsele dynede (the crash in the banqueting-hall): (l.767) at the climax of the battle the poet allows us to view the scene from the Danish viewpoint, namely at a safe distance outside. This technique underlines the violence of the fight as we see and hear Heorot resound and shake

liges faethm (the embraces of fire): (l.781) this is another hint that Heorot will later be destroyed by fire (l.82)

ealde lafe (ancestral swords): (l.795) literally, 'ancient heirlooms'. The Germanic warrior's sword was often an heirloom, sometimes thought to have magical power and, as will be seen later, was of great symbolic importance

ellorgast (the eldritch): (l.807) literally, 'the alien spirit', Grendel

on feonda geweald (into the fiend's domain): (l.808) on his death Grendel returns to the power of the devil. There are many hints at his demonic nature and the fact that he has a soul to lose

Beowulf's victory — lines 825−867

Beowulf has cleansed Heorot from evil and in so doing has accomplished his boast. He hangs up Grendel's severed limb as a trophy and chieftains come from afar to track Grendel's footprints. He has staggered to the mere where he had his lair, dived in and died. His soul has gone to hell. Beowulf's heroic deed is proclaimed by all and there is great rejoicing.

NOTES AND GLOSSARY:

gefaelsod (cleansed): (l.825) Beowulf is seen as a saviour who purifies Heorot from evil

gilp gelaested (made good his boast): (l.829) an important point

tacen (signal): (l.833) Grendel's arm becomes a symbol of defeated evil. Later it is replaced by the monster's head

brim (tarn): (l.847) the lake or mere under which Grendel lived

haethene sawle (heathen soul): (l.852) this stresses the fact that he is not only a monster but also a malevolent force. It is therefore fitting that he has his abode in an underground, dark cave

lines 862−3: the poet is at pains to clear Hrothgar of any blame and to ensure that the Danish king is not slighted

The stories of Sigemund and Heremod — lines 867−915

A Danish poet composes a heroic song in praise of Beowulf, comparing him to the great dragon-slayer Sigemund and contrasting him with the evil king Heremod.

NOTES AND GLOSSARY:

Hrothgar's *scop* or poet creates a new song, this time in praise of Beowulf's deeds. This highlights the importance of the *scop*, literally 'the creator', who could orally compose a lay that fits the situation. His services would help ensure the immortality of the hero, and in a pre-Christian society this would have been vital. The poet takes words and phrases out of his 'storehouse' of verses and can *wordum wrixlan*, 'vary the phrases'; this is a reference to the oral formulaic method of composition and the poetic device of variation.

Sigemund: (l.875) son of Waels and uncle of Fitela. By immediately following the eulogy on Beowulf with the story of a famous Germanic hero, Sigemund, the poet pays Beowulf a great compliment. Traditionally it is Sigurd who is the illustrious dragon-slayer, but in the English tradition Sigemund and his son Sigurd are confused. Mention of a dragon-slayer also prepares us for Beowulf's final battle with the dragon. The audience might also have known that the gold Sigurd took from the dragon had a curse on it which led to his death; this would tragically anticipate Beowulf's own death

Heremod: (l.901) a mythical ruler of the Danes. Having praised Beowulf by comparing him to a great hero, the *scop* now contrasts him with an evil king who is mean, cruel and mad. The duties of kingship are also outlined and the example of Heremod is to be given later in Hrothgar's 'sermon'

Hrothgar's speech of thanks and Beowulf's reply   lines 916−979

Hrothgar gives thanks to God for the great victory and adopts Beowulf as a son in addition to giving him much treasure. He also assures Beowulf that his name will live in eternal honour. Beowulf gives a résumé of the fight and pronounces Denmark free from Grendel's tyranny.

NOTES AND GLOSSARY:

Alwealdan (Governor of all): (l.928) God. The epithets for God and Hrothgar vary according to their present function. Hrothgar first thanks God for this miracle

bote (remedy): (l.934) Beowulf's act is seen in medical terms as a cure for evil

maegtha (she): (l.943) literally, 'maiden'; this refers to Beowulf's mother. There are echoes here of the Virgin Mary (see the Bible, Luke 11:27)

for sunu (as a son): (l.947) Hrothgar pays Beowulf the highest compliment of 'adopting' him as a son—not necessarily in the full legal sense

thin dom lyfath (undying honour): (l.954) it is the greatest possible praise to a Germanic warrior to suggest that he has achieved immortal glory

synnum geswenced (laden with sins): (l.975) this stresses the human nature of Grendel; for example, Beowulf mentions 'sins', 'guilty criminal' and God's judgement, while Grendel is called *guma, maga*—words for 'man'

miclan domes (a greater judgement): (l.978) the Last Judgement when Christ will judge all mankind

---

Celebreations at Heorot   lines 980−1062

All stare in wonder at Grendel's arm and a great feast is prepared in Heorot which has its walls hung with tapestries. Hrothgar enters and celebrations begin with the bestowing of treasure on Beowulf. Hrothgar's open-handedness also extends to Beowulf's followers and compensation is made for the dead Geat.

NOTES AND GLOSSARY:

sunu Ecglafes (The son of Edgelaf): (l.980) Unferth, who is now silent

gestsele (guest-hall): (l.994) Heorot is now transformed into a courtly, festive building, thus reverting to its original function as the centre of an orderly civilisation and where gifts are dispensed

lines 1002–8: this is one of the many moralising or gnomic passages. The poet broadens his comments on Grendel's inability to avoid death to include all mankind who must die after the feast (of life). It is not specifically a Christian sentiment: afterlife is described as a sleep

Hrothulf: (l.1017) one of Hrothgar's nephews. There is a strong hint here and in Queen Wealhtheow's later speech that Hrothulf presents a danger to Hrothgar's sons' succession

facenstafas (falsity): (l.1018) the poet sinisterly hints that there was no treachery in those days. This is another example of tragic anticipation of future disaster at the height of celebrations

ne gefraegn ic (I have not heard): (l.1027) a common rhetorical device in epic poetry

helmes hrof (crown of the helmet): (l.1030) the description of the helmet reminds one of the finds at Sutton Hoo (see pages 74–6)

eodor Ingwina (The Protector of the Sons of Scyld): (l.1044) Ingwine refers to the Danes, Ing being an ancient god. Hrothgar here is alluded to in a series of magnificent titles so he is not overshadowed by Beowulf

hordweard (guardian of the treasures): (l.1047) Hrothgar's function of disperser of the treasure and his open-handedness are emphasised

yrfelafe (an old thing of beauty): (l.1053) literally, 'heirloom'. These heirlooms are not to be hoarded but used; they accumulate a reputation that reflects their owners

lines 1056–62: God appears here to control Fate. This implies a divine providence as opposed to a fatalistic view of life which appears elsewhere in the poem (for example, l.455)

The tale of Finn   lines 1063−1162

Hrothgar's bard sings the tale of Finn. The poet assumes that his audience knows the details and background, as much is omitted. The bard
concentrates on Hildeburh and in so doing stresses the tragic elements.
Hildeburh, daughter of Hoc of the Half-Danes (a branch of the Danish
royal family) marries Finn, king of the Frisians. They belong to races
that have hitherto been at war. Hildeburh's brother, Hnaef, with a
group of Danes visits her; a quarrel breaks out between the two groups
of warriors and Hnaef and Hildeburh's son are killed in a night attack.
Finn also suffers a loss of men.

An uneasy truce is made because of the winter and Hengest takes on
the leadership of the Half-Danes. Finn assumes the role of ring-giver in
this artificial situation and both parties swear oaths not to attack the
other in spite of the fact that vengeance is demanded. There is a moving
scene in which Hildeburh sings a lament at the funeral pyre of her
brother and son. Hengest, however, plans revenge and in the spring the
Danes are reinforced. Finn and his men are killed in their hall and
Hildeburh is returned to her own people.

NOTES AND GLOSSARY:
See Part 3, Commentary, p.78.

gomenwudu (lute): (l.1065) literally, 'playing wood'. There is a recon-
struction of a *scop*'s lute in the Sutton Hoo collec-
tion. The heroic lays were apparently accompanied

Eotena treowe (the good faith of the Jutes): (l.1072) it is not certain
who is referred to here. If the Jutes are the Fris-
ians, then full blame is placed on Finn. It is possible that they are a third tribe, temporarily under
Finn's protection like the Half-Danes; Finn would
then be less culpable and the tragedy the greater

lindplegan (linden-wood clash): (l.1073) a clash of shields (made of
linden wood)

Hoces dohtor (daughter of Hoc): (l.1076) Hildeburh

Folcwaldan sunu (the son of Folcwalda): (l.1089) Finn

lines 1102−6:   this stresses the impossible and frustrating situation both sides find themselves in. The Danes obey
their deceased lord's killer

Ad (pyre):   (l.1107) the fire on which the dead were to be
cremated. This is the way Beowulf's funeral will be
conducted

Ides gnornode (she sang the dirges): (l.1117) this is in keeping with
funeral custom. At Beowulf's funeral a woman
loudly sings a lament

holm storme weol (the boiling ocean): (l.1131) the nature imagery here, as is usual in Old English poetry, reflects the mood of the scene

wrecca (exile): (l.1137) Hengest

Hunlafing (the son of Hunlaf): (l.1143) one of Hnaef's warriors. He places a sword across Hengest's knees to remind him of the need for revenge and to show his will-ingness to give support

Guthlaf ond Oslaf: (l.1148) followers of Hnaef and Hengest, perhaps reinforcements for the revenge mission

Sceotend Scyldinga (The Scylding crewmen): (l.1154) the Danish war-riors; they carry back Finn's treasures with Hilde-burh

gleomannes gyd (gleeman's lay): (l.1160) the song of the poet-singer

---

Wealhtheow's speech   lines 1163–1231

Hrothgar's queen, Wealhtheow, approaches the throne and dispenses wine. She urges her husband to be generous to Beowulf but discreetly suggests that, although Beowulf is adopted as a son, Hrothgar should not forget their own children Hrethric and Hrothmund, who ought to inherit the kingdom. She trusts that Hrothulf, the King's nephew, will guard the boys if Hrothgar should die prematurely. The cup is then passed to Beowulf who is given more treasure, including a collar. The later, tragic history of this collar is narrated: Hygelac, Beowulf's king, will wear it in a battle he provokes against the Frisians. Wealhtheow asks Beowulf to protect her sons.

NOTES AND GLOSSARY:
This section, following the Finn episode which also has a queen at the centre, is steeped in subtle innuendo. Although the mood changes from the chaos and treachery of the Danish-Frisian battle to the harmony of the peace-weaver, Wealhtheow, we are made aware of hidden tensions at Hrothgar's court. Wealhtheow fears Hrothulf's ambition to usurp her sons' right to the throne.

suhtergefaederan (uncle and nephew): (l.1164) Hrothgar and Hrothulf. By stating that they were faithful *at that time* implies further disaster. See the comments on ll.1017–18. Beowulf's 'cleansing' of the hall does not purify internal conflict, and even his great deed leads to Grendel's mother's attack

Unferth: (l.1165) the seating arrangements are interesting here. Hrothgar is flanked by two potentially sus-pect counsellors, one a 'peace-breaker'

glaedne Hrothulf (gracious Hrothulf): (l.1181) Wealhtheow's speech is very diplomatic and subtle. She praises her husband, urges him to consider the position of their children, and appeals to both Hrothulf and Beowulf for support. The speech shows her political insight

Hrethric ond Hrothmund: (l.1189) Wealhtheow's sons; they probably sit at a lower bench because they are younger than Hrothulf and Unferth

healsbeaga maest (the richest collar): (l.1195) a very precious necklace or torque. The digression on the necklace adds a note of treachery to the scene. (See pp.72−3)

Brosinga mene (the Brising necklace): (l.1199) the gift reminds the poet of this famous necklace. Again the poet expects the audience to know about it; Hama appears to have stolen it from the Gothic tyrant Eormenric, famed for his treachery. The story is one of deceit and underlines the queen's fears of future treachery in the Danish court

thone hring (This gold): (l.1202) the necklace Beowulf has just received. It also has a tragic future in store, because of pride and treachery

getheoh tela (May fortune come with them): (l.1218) again an ironic remark, as we already know that bad fortune comes with the necklace

lines 1226−31: Wealhtheow's praise and good wishes are couched in requests for future help. The final section on openness and truthfulness in Heorot must be highly ironic

---

Grendel's mother attacks   lines 1232−1309

The feast continues and none knows what is destined to happen that night. The benches are replaced by beds and the warriors retire. Grendel's mother approaches, intent on revenge. The poet recounts again the great struggle between Beowulf and Grendel. The new monster enters Heorot and the warriors grab their armour; Grendel's mother quickly escapes, but not before grabbing Ashhere, Hrothgar's counsellor and friend. She takes his body and Grendel's arm back to her lair. Sorrow returns to Heorot and Hrothgar laments anew.

NOTES AND GLOSSARY:

Wyrd ne cuthon (the weird they did not know): (l.1233) they were unaware of the fate that awaited them. Again a hint of approaching disaster in the middle of rejoicing

Sum sare angeald (A savage penalty one paid): (l.1251) this refers to Ashhere who will be killed

wrecend (an avenger): (l.1256) Grendel's mother. By stressing her function as an avenger the poet gives her good reason for attack

Cain: (l.1261) see the note on l.107

geosceaftgasta (the ill ones): (l.1266) literally, 'demons sent by fate' (Klaeber)

haeletha leofost (the hero): (l.1296) Ashhere

cuthe folme (the hand . . . familiar): (l.1303) Grendel's arm that was hung up in the hall

---

Beowulf is summoned by Hrothgar   lines 1310–1382

Hrothgar is in despair, summons Beowulf and relates the events of the previous night. Now that Ashhere is dead many thanes will be lordless. Hrothgar vividly describes the monsters and their abode, an evil and frightening region, windy, frosty, dark and mysterious. The pure hart would rather die than swim in the evil water to escape capture. Hrothgar promises Beowulf a great reward if he can find a remedy.

NOTES AND GLOSSARY:

frean Ingwina (Guide of the Ingwine): (l.1319) Hrothgar. Ingwine means 'friends of Ing', a term for the Danes

aefter neod-lathum (after a call so urgent): (l.1320) Beowulf has been sleeping elsewhere and is surprised by the alarm

Sorh is geniwod (Woe has returned): (l.1322) this is a stock expression that emphasises the constant flux of sorrow and joy (for another example, see l.1775, 'grief sprang from joy')

faehthe wraec (taken vengeance): (l.1333) Hrothgar frequently repeats the fact that Grendel's mother is following the rules of the Germanic code by seeking revenge

lines 1343–4: 'the hand' refers to Ashhere, the high-ranking lord unable to distribute treasure and give protection now

ellorgaestas (otherworldly ones): (l.1349) Grendel and his mother. We have no description of their physical appearance, other than size, but their evil nature is repeatedly mentioned

wraeclastas traed (trod also the tracks of exile): (l.1352) this stresses their state of exile from society

dygel lond (Mysterious is the region): (l.1357) literally, 'secret country'. In this vivid passage (ll.1357−76) the poet creates an atmosphere of eery mystery, suspense and fear. There are echoes of *The Vision of St Paul*, an early medieval account of a descent into hell. The section evokes images of hell, chaos and terror that set the scene for Beowulf's second battle

aer he feorh seleth (he will sell it on the brink): (l.1370) literally, 'he will sooner give up his spirit [i.e. die]' than enter the evil water

---

Beowulf exhorts Hrothgar   lines 1383−1441

Beowulf encourages Hrothgar to be less pessimistic and more active. A warrior must always be daring if he is to be remembered. He makes a promise to rid Denmark of this monster. Hrothgar's courage is renewed and he rides out with Beowulf and his men where they see traces of Ashhere's blood in the water and his head nearby. They sound the war horn and the mass of evil sea snakes and monsters becomes enraged. Beowulf kills one of them and his men take it out of the water and examine it.

NOTES AND GLOSSARY:

lines 1384−9: Beowulf's speech is a typical heroic exhortation to conceal sorrow and to act courageously in order to achieve *dom*, 'glory' or 'renown'. It sums up the 'pagan consolation', that a heroic and glorious life alone can give immortality. Reputation is all

thone selestan (the best man): (l.1406) Ashhere

fyrdleoth (battle cry): (l.1424) the poet goes into conventional Old English battle description here, although no battle takes place

on seglrade (in the seas): (l.1429) literally, 'sail-road'. The poet lists all the evil sea monsters in the mere (compare ll.422 and 558). There is the suggestion here, as was common in the Middle Ages, that all sea beasts were evil. A source for such belief was the evil Leviathan in the Bible (Job 41:1). Beowulf's battle is seen to be against evil itself and his victory one that saves all sailors

waegbora (strange lurker of the waves): (l.1440) this is the sea monster Beowulf shoots. Just as Grendel's mother took Ashhere, so Beowulf takes a sacrificial victim

The armouring scene   lines 1441–1491

Beowulf's armour is put on: a mailed shirt that would allow no harm to come to him, a shining helmet with boar motifs that no sword could cut through, and a famous sword, Hrunting, that Unferth lends him. This sword had never failed anyone. Unferth would not himself go with Beowulf and thereby he lost his reputation. Beowulf asks Hrothgar to protect his troops if he should be killed and to send the treasure Hrothgar gave him to Hygelac, so that the value of Beowulf's acts will be recognised in his home country.

NOTES AND GLOSSARY:

herebyrne (mailed shirt): (l.1443) unlike in earlier battles Beowulf now requires armour. It gives the poet a chance to describe the armour and sword which are personified in this passage. It is implied that they provide magical protection (see ll.1446ff.)

hwita helm (silver helmet): (l.1448) this sounds like the helmets found in royal burial mounds. The boar was a royal symbol, and it appears as if there was a border round the helmet with boars engraved on it

Hrunting: (l.1457) Unferth's hereditary sword

atertanum fah (annealed in venom): (l.1459) this could either mean that the sword was stained with poison to make a wound lethal or that acid was used to make the design on the blade, the 'wave-patterned sword' of l.1489

mago Ecglafes (son of Edgelaf): (l.1465) Unferth. He is generous to give Beowulf his sword, although he is seen to be cowardly here (ll.1468–71)

sunu Hraedles (Hrethel's son): (l.1485) King Hygelac of Geatland. As one's reputation determines one's afterlife, Beowulf is eager that his own people be aware of the magnitude of his acts of heroism, and this can be gauged by the value of Hrothgar's gifts

widcuthne man (a widely-known man): (l.1489) Unferth, to whom Beowulf gives his sword in a generous gesture

The fight with Grendel's mother   lines 1492–1590

Beowulf dives underwater and journeys down for the greater part of a day until he sees the foot of the mere. Grendel's mother grabs him but cannot penetrate his armour; as she takes him to her lair he is attacked by mobs of sea monsters. Beowulf deals her a great blow but his sword is useless for the first time in its history. He throws away the sword and determines to use his bare hands. They wrestle furiously and Grendel's mother draws her knife but cannot pierce Beowulf's armour. God comes to Beowulf's assistance; he sees an ancient giant sword in the cave that no other man could bear, and with it he deals the monster such a blow on her neck that she dies. By the help of a light in the cave Beowulf examines the place, finds Grendel's body and severs the head.

NOTES AND GLOSSARY:

hwil daeges (a day's space): (l.1495) a typical heroic exaggeration, as in the Breca incident

atolan clommum (her terrible hooks): (l.1502) Grendel's mother uses the same method as her son, namely her hand grip

nithsele (enemy hall): (l.1513) Grendel's lair is called a hall, but is described as a hell opposed to the paradisal Heorot. The description is traditional in Germanic legend for a monster's home

beadoleoma (battle-flame): (l.1523) literally, 'battle light'; it refers to the sword Hrunting which would have flashed as he flourished it. As in the fight with Grendel all swords are useless against a monster, except her own sword which he later uses

his dom alaeg (betrayed its name): (l.1528) literally, 'its glory failed'

lines 1534–6: a gnomic or moralising passage that stresses the hero's need to persevere to achieve eternal glory. This carelessness for one's life is compatible with Christian teaching

lines 1541–4: one critic, E.B. Irving, stresses the reciprocal nature of events: his sword fails, her knife fails; he throws her, she throws him, and so on. This stresses the evenness of both sides and the importance of divine intervention. See Irving's *A Reading of Beowulf*, Yale University Press, New Haven, Conn., 1968, pp.122–3

seax (knife): (l.1545) this suggests her human nature

ealdsweord eotenisc (a Giant-sword from former days): (l.1558) ancient weapons were considered to have mystical powers and were often accredited to giants. Such a conveniently placed weapon is also found in other heroic tales

aenig mon other (no other man): (l.1560) the reader is reminded of Arthur's sword Excalibur which only he could own

lines 1563–9: the short, sharp bursts of action are reflected in the abrupt versification and the accumulation of active verbs

rodores candel (the candle of heaven): (l.1572) a kenning for the sun. After the battle the cave is filled with light

heafde becearf (he had severed the head): (l.1590) apart from trophy-hunting it has been suggested that Beowulf's act prevents the ghost of Grendel haunting Heorot

---

Beowulf's triumphant return   lines 1591–1676

The scene shifts to the spectators at the edge of the mere who see the blood rising to the surface. Hrothgar returns home, sure of Beowulf's failure, but the Geats have faith in their lord. The blade of the giant sword Beowulf found in the cave melts like ice in the spring and he takes the remaining hilt and the head of Grendel with him, leaving all other treasure. Now the waters are cleansed and Beowulf swims to the surface where he is met by his loyal thanes. The fourteen Geats joyfully return to Heorot with the head of Grendel which they proudly display to the Danes. Beowulf narrates the adventure to Hrothgar and gives thanks to God. Now they are again free from troubles and Denmark cleansed of evil.

NOTES AND GLOSSARY:

non-daeges (the ninth hour): (l.1600) the church's service at 3 p.m., called None

goldwine gumena (the kindly gold-giver): (l.1602) Hrothgar, who has no faith that Beowulf will return

Gistas (foreigners): (l.1602) the Geats who remain. They are active, optimistic, while the Danes are fatalistic

wigbil (war-tool): (l.1607) the giant sword whose blade melts after its function is over, as Arthur's Excalibur disappears. The dragon in the Sigemund episode also melted away (l.897)

ise gelicost (like the ice): (l.1608) the simile of ice melting in spring prepares us for the new, joyous season at Heorot when hope is renewed. The image stresses the cyclical nature of joy and tragedy in the world, yet all, the poet stresses, is in God's hands (ll.1609–11)

hilt: (l.1614) the ornamented hilt of the sword does not melt

ellorgaest (the fiend): (l.1617) presumably Grendel, not his mother

lidmanna helm (the seamen's Helm): (l.1623) Beowulf is here described as the Guardian of the sailors, because of his cleansing of the seas from monsters (ll.1618–22)

lines 1623–50:   in this passage the manly, rejoicing Geats are subtly constrasted with the escapist, drinking Danes, who must have been shocked by the abrupt entry of the Geats with Grendel's head held aloft; compare the Green Knight's entry into Arthur's hall in *Sir Gawain and the Green Knight*

ylda Waldend (the Guide of mankind): (l.1661) God, whom Beowulf immediately acknowledges as his guardian

---

The history of the sword   lines 1677–1698

The poet tells the history of the giant sword found in the cave. It has been made by a giant, owned by monsters and now is in the keeping of the Danish king. On the hilt was engraved the story of the Flood that killed the giants and on the cross-piece in runic letters the name of the warrior for whom it was forged.

NOTES AND GLOSSARY:
The sword's origins go back to the beginning of the world when there were giants (see the Bible, Genesis 6:4 and ll.111–14 of *Beowulf*). The sword bears witness to the destruction of all evil at the Flood, and this foreshadows its present use when Beowulf purges evil in his underwater battle. Now its function is over and it remains an object of beauty with the carved hilt alone surviving.

deofla hryre (the fall of demons): (l.1680) Grendel and his mother

or writen (The spring was cut): (l.1688) literally, 'the beginning [origin of the primeval strife] was engraved'. Possibly designs of the Flood were depicted

runstafas (runic letters): (l.1695) the Old Norse script

hwam (for whose sake): (l.1696) it was common to have the first owner's name engraved on the cross-piece of the hilt

---

Hrothgar's 'sermon'   lines 1698–1784

Hrothgar's speech is in three parts. He starts by praising Beowulf for his heroism and modesty, contrasting him to the mean and cruel King Heremod. The second section comprises a sermon on God's Providence; how God gives power, wisdom and land, ensuring that all will go well. The danger is that such a ruler becomes proud, slothful and dissatisfied, forgetting his God-given gifts. He will then be overthrown and another will take his place as treasure-giver. Beowulf is urged to reject all pride, for although he is at present at the height of his strength, one day sickness, battle, flames or flood will carry him off.

The third part is about Hrothgar's own life. He reigned for fifty years until Grendel attacked and joy turned to sorrow. Thank God that that time is no more.

NOTES AND GLOSSARY:
See Part 3, Commentary, pp.69–71, concerning this speech

Heremod: (l.1709) see ll.898–915

lines 1728–34:   God permits man to live in joy and comfort; man's problem is how to use these 'lent' gifts properly

se slaep (That sleep): (l.1742) pride leads to the sin of sloth, spiritual laziness, in which stage one's spiritual 'armour' is weakest and the devil can attack (l.1747). See the Bible, Ephesians 6:13–17

hund missera (for fifty years): (l.1769) this is the same period Beowulf is to reign before his troubles begin

---

Beowulf's farewells   lines 1784–1913

After the feasting the Geats are keen to leave early the next morning. Beowulf returns Hrunting to Unferth and loyally promises to support Hrothgar and Hrethric in the future. Hrothgar praises Beowulf for his wisdom, maturity and strength: the Geats could not find a better king on Hygelac's death, he says. Hrothgar pledges aid and treasure to Beowulf and the Geats, and presents him with twelve more treasures before final farewells are made. The coastguard who first greeted them on their arrival bids them farewell.

NOTES AND GLOSSARY:
Beowulf's behaviour is flawless as a courteous prince as well as a fierce warrior; his speech is gracious and rhetorical and he is particularly diplomatic towards Unferth.

sunu Ecglafes (the son of Edgelaf): (l.1808) Unferth. Beowulf hands back the sword, Hrunting, diplomatically thanking Unferth (although it was useless). This action, and the lack of animosity and censure, would smooth over a potential problem in the future. All Beowulf's actions are aimed at making peace

Hrethric: (l.1836) Beowulf promises future aid to both king and Hrethric, thus acknowledging him as the heir-apparent

Hrethles eaferan (the son of Hrethel): (l.1847) Hygelac. Hrothgar's wish that Hygelac should be succeeded by Beowulf is interesting, as Hygelac has sons whereas Beowulf is only a nephew. The Danish king and queen fear that their nephew will usurp the throne from their sons

ofer ganotes baeth (over the gannet's bath): (l.1861) kenning for the sea

lac ond luftacen (presents and pledges): (l.1863) these are two major elements to create future peace

othres swithor (the second more likely): (l.1874) Hrothgar implies that he will either meet him again or not; the latter was more likely

orleahtre (blameless): (l.1886) the poet is at pains to show that Hrothgar's misfortunes do not stem from any fault. Old age was alone responsible. A central theme of youth contrasted with age is seen here—Beowulf / Hrothgar, and later the thane Beowulf/King Beowulf

Landweard (coastguard): (l.1890) his reappearance rounds off the Danish adventure. Beowulf, like Scyld the mythic hero, comes and leaves Denmark by ship, departing with treasures

batwearde (boat-guard): (l.1900) Beowulf's generous gift and the glimpse we have of the man's future pride in it, show the power of gift-giving and the foresight that goes into proper gift distribution

---

Beowulf returns to Geatland   lines 1914—1998

Beowulf lands in Geatland and has the treasure taken to the great hall where Hygelac and Hygd live. The poet praises Queen Hygd by contrasting her with Offa's cruel queen. Beowulf's arrival is announced and after formal greetings Hygelac eagerly asks Beowulf to tell of his adventures. They give thanks for Beowulf's successful return.

NOTES AND GLOSSARY:

Hygd: (l.1926) Hygelac's queen and daughter of Hareth

Modthrytho: (l.1931) Thryth is the wife of King Offa. As Beowulf was contrasted with Heremod, so Hygd is complimented by contrasting her with his proud queen. It is the traditional 'taming of the shrew' story. We also see the duties and function of a queen in this passage

Hemminges maeg (Hemming's son): (l.1944) Offa. Probably the late fourth-century King Offa of the Angles is intended, the legendary ancestor of King Offa of Mercia (757—96) who may have ruled when this poem was written

Eomer: (l.1960) Offa's son

nefa Garmundes (Garmund's grandson): (l.1962) Garmund is Offa's father

bonan Ongentheoes (Ongentheow's conqueror): (l.1968) Hygelac, whose wars with the Swedish king Ongentheow are narrated later. Hygelac is presented as the perfect, ring-giving king

lines 1994–7: this is the first mention of Hygelac's attempts to dissuade Beowulf from the enterprise. It adds to Beowulf's prestige that he was not sent by Hygelac

---

Beowulf's narration and the story of Freawaru and Ingeld
lines 1999–2069

Beowulf announces that he has successfully cleared Denmark of all monsters and begins to describe his adventures by mentioning the hospitality he received at Heorot. He remembers Hrothgar's daughter Freawaru who was betrothed to Ingeld. This leads him to speculate on the outcome of such a match. Hrothgar hopes to achieve peace by marrying his daughter to a Heathobard, yet Beowulf fears that fresh feuding will ensue. He imagines a scene with Danes and Heathobards at table together, the Danes sporting weapons taken from defeated Heathobards in the past. An older Heathobard might taunt a younger one that a Dane carries his slain father's sword and this will lead to fresh slaughter, culminating in Ingeld's love for Freawaru lessening.

NOTES AND GLOSSARY:
In every retelling of the Grendel episode the poet introduces new material and perspectives. This is a tale of tragedy and feud akin to the Finn episode and stresses that all attempts to ensure future peace are tenuous.

maeru cwen (A noble princess): (l.2016) Freawaru
suna Frodan (son of Froda): (l.2025) Ingeld, son of the chief of the Heathobards. Ingeld would have been well known to the audience from other lays
thaet raed talath (accounts it wisdom): (l.2027) this is a direct criticism of Hrothgar's policy
eald aescwiga (An old spear-fighter): (l.2042) an imagined Heathobard. The importance of the past history of a sword is seen here

---

Beowulf describes his battles
lines 2069–2199

Beowulf continues his narrative of his Danish exploits, adding the facts that the Geat killed by Grendel was called Handscio, and that Grendel had a huge glove or bag of dragon's skin in which he put his prey. He recounts the celebrations at Heorot after Grendel's death, the

attack of Grendel's mother with the death of Ashhere and the final
battle in the mere. The rich gifts from Hrothgar Beowulf hands over to
Hygelac and Hygd receives the necklace Wealhtheow had given Beowulf. Beowulf is highly praised and we learn that he had been under-
rated for a long time by Hygelac and considered lazy. Hygelac bestows
gifts of land, titles and a hall on Beowulf.

NOTES AND GLOSSARY:

Glof (glove): (1.2085) no glove has been mentioned before. Such
a pouch is characteristically the property of trolls

lines 2111–14: the lay which Hrothgar sings stresses the problem
of old age and underlines the theme of age contras-
ted with youth

death werigne (death-wearied dear one): (1.2125) Ashhere. It was a
tragedy not to have the body to bury properly

line 2141: this line implies that Beowulf was not yet fated to die

lines 2148–50: Hrothgar has given Beowulf gifts which 'accorded
to usage' and Beowulf passes them on to his lord.
This shows the normal and expected use of treasure

lyt . . . heafodmaga (Little family): (1.2150) Beowulf's father is not a
Geat, but his maternal grandfather, Hrethel, had
fostered him (see ll.2430–4)

Hiorogar: (1.2158) Hrothgar's elder brother who handed
kingdom and treasure to his younger brother and
not to his son Heoroweard, possibly because
Heoroweard was under age

inwitnet (nets of malice): (1.2167) the threatened malice between uncle
and nephew in Denmark is in sharp contrast with
the loyalty Beowulf shows his uncle

healsbeah (neck-ring): (1.2172) this is the torque mentioned above
(ll.1155ff.). We already know that Hygelac is to
wear it on his death day when he attacks the
Franks. Another sign of the significance of treasure

lines 2177–89: in this passage Beowulf's unpromising youth is
mentioned. This is a typical epic feature and underlines the hero's later grandeur. Heremod started
life promisingly, but ended in disaster

Hrethles lafe (the bequest of Hrethel): (1.2191) the Geatish king's hereditary treasure

---

King Beowulf's reign and the dragon's hoard   lines 2200–2311

The second part of the poem begins with Beowulf as king. He has ruled
for fifty years after the deaths of Hygelac and his son Heardred when

tragedy strikes in the shape of a dragon that ravages the kingdom. A thief had entered the dragon's cave and stolen some treasure; he was an exiled slave who intended winning protection again by giving his master a gift. The treasure had been used in an earlier age by a race that had died out and the last survivor had brought the treasure to that cave. The dragon took over the guardianship of the hoard after the last survivor's death and kept it for three hundred years until this theft. The slave achieves his aim but the theft awakens the dragon's anger.

NOTES AND GLOSSARY:
As the poet concentrates on Beowulf's three fights, we silently pass over fifty years until old age has also come to Beowulf, who reigns success-fully, like Hrothgar, until tragedy strikes. The poet seems to stress the innocence of all parties involved: it was common knowledge that a dra-gon's duty was to guard treasure, and he does so without any violence until provoked, while the slave's reason for the theft is also understand-able—he requires some gift in order to re-enter society. The poet also tells us the history of the treasure to show its innocence also; it had served a great race that had died out through no fault of its own. The brevity of civilisations, as well as the life of the individual, is thus stressed.

Heardred: (1.2202) Hygelac's son who is killed by the Scyl-fings, that is, the Swedes (1.2205). The details of Hygelac's and Heardred's deaths are given later in flashbacks

nefan Hererices (Hereric's nephew): (1.2206) Heardred; Hereric may be Queen Hygd's brother

stanbeorh (barrow): (1.2213) a burial chamber, covered with earth. It was considered the natural function of a dragon to guard treasure. In the Old English *Maxims*—a col-lection of gnomic sentiments—we find 'The dragon shall dwell in the cave, old, splendid in ornaments'

nathwylc (one man): (1.2215) literally, 'someone or other', the slave

threanedlan (necessity): (1.2223) the poet stresses the slave's need to steal. He does achieve pardon, probably from one of Beowulf's thanes, for the cup passes into Beo-wulf's own possession (1.2404)

on geardagum (In another age): (1.2232) the poet discusses the uses and abuses of treasure which shares the fate of its owners. The race and this treasure are 'death-rapt' now. The treasure's devalued state is seen in the rust and in its inability to serve any function

hringa hyrde (The keeper of rings): (1.2245) refers to the sole survivor who hid the treasure and awaits the fate of his fel-lows

lines 2247−66: this is a typical Old English elegy, such as is found in poems like *The Seafarer* (compare ll.2444ff.). Such verse normally ends with the Christian consolation that worldly transience is followed by eternal joy in heaven, but no such consolation is here

guthdeath (war-death): (l.2249) the survivor stresses the fact that his tribe was not cowardly, but subject to natural law; compare Hrothgar's speech, ll.1758−68. There is also a tragic anticipation here of the fate of the Geats: Beowulf will possess the stolen cup, the treasure will lead to his death and be placed in his burial mound, and then his race will be subject to 'war-death' as well

friothowaere (peace-offering): (l.2282) ironically the slave uses the treasure for its true purpose—to give as a gift to ensure peace and protection

unfaege (undoomed): (l.2291) refers to the slave who survives the ordeal, because not yet 'doomed'. Here God and fate seem to be the same (compare ll.572−3)

sincgifan (treasure-giver): (l.2311) Beowulf. We are told already that Beowulf is not to survive this affair

---

The dragon's attacks   lines 2312−2354

The dragon attacks everything in his nightly visits, before retreating to his cave at dawn. Beowulf's hall itself is burned down and the king plunged into despair and feelings of guilt. He plans to fight the dragon and has an iron shield made for himself. Both will die in the fight, we are told. Beowulf will fight alone, trusting in his strength.

NOTES AND GLOSSARY:
Beowulf immediately thinks, unlike Hrothgar, that the dragon's attacks are an act of God's retribution, but, unlike Hrothgar, Beowulf decides to act swiftly.

seo wen (his faith): (l.2323) we are shown, as with Grendel, how he is misled in his sense of security, because of pride

his sylfes ham (his own hall): (l.2325) Beowulf's own hall is burned down—a worse fate than Hrothgar's. As the hall symbolises the nation, this might be a forewarning of the calamity facing the entire race

wende se wisa (The chieftain supposed): (l.2329) Beowulf's immediate reaction is to blame himself; this implies a belief in the principle of cause and effect, but he is at present unaware of the dragon's motives

guthkyning (formidable king): (l.2335) literally, 'war-king'. The titles used for Beowulf in this section are significant: he is *wisa* (l.2329), 'one who shows the way'; *wigendra hleo* (l.2337), 'champion of warriors'; *sincgifan* (l.2311), 'treasure-giver'; *hringa fengel* (l.2345), 'prince of rings' (suggesting his correct use of rings)

laendaga (transitory world): (l.2341) literally, 'transitory days'. Both the brief nature of man's life and the fact that Beowulf's days are numbered are suggested here

Flashback to Heardred's reign	lines 2354—2390

The poet fills in part of the Geats' history which was previously omitted. Hygelac was killed by the Frisians but Beowulf escaped by virtue of his swimming powers. Queen Hygd offered Beowulf the throne, but he refused to let her son Heardred be passed over. He protects Heardred who is later killed by Onela of Sweden. Heardred had given protection to Ohthere's sons, Eanmund and Eadgils, who fought their uncle Onela. Onela takes revenge on Heardred and Beowulf is left as ruler of the Geats.

NOTES AND GLOSSARY:
For the events in the two Swedish Wars, see Part 3, Commentary, pp.68—9.

This section is the first of a series of flashbacks concerning the turbulent events that lead to Beowulf's succession. These sections create suspense as we await the great dragon battle and they show the fateful and tragic past history of the Geats. It also strengthens the fear that the Swedes will attack Geatland on Beowulf's death.

Freslondum (Friesland): (l.2357) the ill-advised battle against the Frisians is described in ll.1202ff., although there is no word of criticism of Hygelac here. Beowulf is not directly connected with this ill-fated expedition, and escapes by swimming

Hetware: (l.2363) a Frankish tribe

Hygd: (l.2369) Hygelac's queen does not have faith in her young son Heardred and presses Beowulf to become king. By refusing Beowulf attempts to avoid future problems and again proves the perfect thane. The tension between uncle and nephew (or in Beowulf's case, cousins), is seen in the Hrothgar-Hrothulf and Onela-Eadgils problems. Beowulf places national peace above personal ambition

wraecmaecgas (outcasts from overseas): (l.2379) Eanmund and Eadgils. See pages 68–9 for an explanation of this affair

leodhryres (his lord's death): (l.2391) refers to Heardred's death that Beowulf will avenge

---

Beowulf plots the attack   lines 2391–2424

Beowulf takes eleven companions to the dragon's cave, unwillingly guided by the slave who stole the cup. Beowulf encourages his men, but his life is coming to an end, the poet forewarns us.

NOTES AND GLOSSARY:

threotteotha secg (the thirteenth man): (l.2406) the slave

gomelan (the old man): (l.2421) Beowulf is now described, like Hrothgar in the first part, as an old man; this is in sharp contrast to the first part of the story

---

Beowulf recounts the recent history of the Geats   lines 2425–2509

Beowulf recalls how King Hrethel, his grandfather, brought him up as a son along with his uncles Herebeald, Hathkin and Hygelac.

Herebeald is accidentally shot by a stray arrow from his brother Hathkin's bow. This death, being an accident, cannot be avenged and King Hrethel greatly grieves over the tragedy. All joy goes out of his life and all laughter and song until he dies of grief.

Hrethel becomes king and the Swedish wars resume. Ohthere and Onela, sons of King Ongentheow of Sweden, attack and Hathkin is killed, but Eofor avenges his lord and kills Ongentheow. Hygelac now reigns and Beowulf aids him. After Hygelac is killed by Dayraven, champion of the Franks, Beowulf avenges his death.

NOTES AND GLOSSARY:

lines 2441–3:   such a situation is possibly the most tragic conceivable in heroic society. Death must be avenged, but here the father cannot kill his son's slayer. Perhaps a flaw in the heroic code is pointed out here

lines 2444–62:   this is an extended simile in which the poet compares Hrethel's grief to that of a man whose son is hanged. There is no remedy for either. The rhetorical style here is like that of an elegy in which an atmosphere of despair and joylessness is created

Wedra helm (the Helm of the Geats): (l.2462) Hrethel

Ongentheowes eaferan (The sons of Ongentheow): (l.2475) Ohthere and Onela attack a weakened Geatland after Hrethel's death

Eofor: (l.2486) the Geatish warrior who kills Ongentheow (see ll.2961ff.). He is married to Hygelac's daughter

geald aet guthe (to make return): (l.2491) Hygelac is now king and gives Beowulf land and treasure. Beowulf makes return by fighting for Hygelac; this is the true lord-thane relationship

Daeghrefne (Dayraven): (l.2501) the Frank who killed Hygelac. We hear later that Beowulf took his sword, Nailing, from him (l.2680)

hildegrap (handgrasp): (l.2507) literally, 'hostile grasp'. This battle reminds one of Beowulf's earlier hand-to-hand conflicts

---

Beowulf's boast and the dragon fight　　　　　lines 2510–2723

Beowulf explains that armour will be necessary in this fight in which he alone will be involved. He makes a firm oath to carry out this mission. He sees fire issuing from the cave as he gives a challenging cry which enrages the dragon. The shield and sword, we hear, are not going to protect him. Beowulf strikes with his sword but this does not kill the dragon which retaliates and Beowulf is wounded by the fire. Beowulf's men see their leader's plight and flee to the woods, all except Wiglaf who remembers Beowulf's favours and comes to his lord's assistance. We hear the story of Wiglaf's sword.

Wiglaf rebukes his companions for cowardice before he joins Beowulf, whom he encourages. Beowulf makes a fresh attack but his sword fails as 'his hand was too strong'. In return the dragon bites Beowulf's neck which bleeds badly. Wiglaf mortally wounds the dragon and Beowulf gives a final stab with a knife. Beowulf feels the poison in him and knows his time is short. Wiglaf bathes Beowulf's wound and undoes his armour.

NOTES AND GLOSSARY:

Metod (master): (l.2527) *Metod* often refers to God. The poet may be equating God with Fate or he may refer to destiny as our lord/master

lines 2532–3: Beowulf stresses that he will fight alone. There is some discrepancy here with the later reproaches for not helping

guthcyning (warrior-king): (l.2563) Beowulf, unlike Hrothgar, is seen to be both warrior and ruler

lines 2570–5: Beowulf is now doomed to die, fate was not with him and the shield's protection was shorter than he had desired, while the sword bites less strongly than is necessary

guthbill geswac (his good old sword ... failed him): (l.2584) the sword lets him down, as occurred in the fight with Grendel's mother when Hrunting failed

lines 2586–91: the journey refers to death, when he will travel from this world to elsewhere. The poet is deliberately vague about the nature of the next world

aer (former): (l.2595) Beowulf is already described as a past ruler

in anum (of one man): (l.2599) Wiglaf. He enters the scene as the one just man, and has much in common with Beowulf

Weoxstan: (l.2602) Wiglaf's father is a Waymunding, as are Beowulf and his father

Scylfing: (l.2603) Weoxstan is called a Scylfing, that is, a Swede. We can assume that the Waymundings lived on the Geatland-Swedish border. Weoxstan supported the Swede Onela and the Geats backed the other side in this internal Swedish dispute. Onela kills Heardred, while Weoxstan kills Eanmund. It is curious that a prime mover in the side that the Geats oppose, Weoxstan, should finally find shelter in Geatland and his son be a lord of that realm. Beowulf confirms Wiglaf in his father's rich possessions and there is no word of criticism of Weoxstan. He is a thane who loyally serves his lord

ealdsweord etonisc (the ancient giant sword): (l.2616) Eanmund had been killed by Wiglaf's father. There is also tragic irony in the history of this sword: it passes from the slain Eanmund to his slayer, Weoxstan, and thence to Wiglaf who aids Eanmund's earlier protector, Beowulf

geongan cempan (youthful warrior): (l.2625) Wiglaf. He is seen as a novice here, like the young Beowulf

we geheton (we bound ourselves): (l.2634) Wiglaf's speech shows the highest heroic valour: he remembers heroic boasts and promises, he wishes to repay his ring-giving lord and he will die rather than fail

Leofa Biowulf (Beloved Beowulf): (l.2663) this speech seems unnecessary with Beowulf in pain, but the poet stresses the need for a hero never to relax his efforts if he wishes to achieve everlasting reputation

Naegling (Nailing): (l.2680) Beowulf's own sword. Like Hrunting earlier it fails Beowulf who is too strong to wield it. This is typical in Germanic folk tales

secg on searwum (the brave soldier): (l.2700) Wiglaf. There is some confusion as to who actually kills the dragon. It would appear they both do so: the dragon gives Beowulf a deadly bite, Wiglaf deals the decisive stroke and Beowulf follows this up with a knife wound

Wiglaf brings out the treasure   lines 2724–2782

Beowulf realises that he is fatally wounded and death is near. He looks back on his successful fifty years as ruler and comforts himself that he has done all things correctly. He asks Wiglaf to bring the treasure out of the cave so he can see it before he dies. The fabulous treasure is described. Wiglaf sees a standard woven in gold that gives out light.

NOTES AND GLOSSARY:
Beowulf makes a final speech in which he makes Wiglaf his heir, as he has no son. His career resembles Hrothgar's—fifty years of peace before tragedy strikes. His desire to see the treasure is understandable and not a sign of covetousness. He wishes to see what he is dying for and this gold is in a sense his 'man-price', the compensation his country has from his slayer (ll.2799–2801).

oferhigian (get the better of): (l.2766) this theme is found in Hrothgar's 'sermon' when the dangers of pride and avarice are stressed
segn eallgylden (a standard . . . in gold): (l.2767) Grendel's cave was also filled with light after Beowulf's victory

Beowulf's final speech   lines 2783–2820

Wiglaf returns to Beowulf with the treasure and the king makes his final speech. He gives thanks to God that he can acquire this treasure for his people, hands over responsibility to Wiglaf and requests a tomb to be built by the sea as a sign to his people and to seamen. He gives his collar, armour and his authority to Wiglaf, the last of the Waymundings. His soul then leaves his body for the fate of the righteous.

NOTES AND GLOSSARY:
Hronesnaesse (Whale's Headland): (l.2805) the tomb he has in mind is a burial mound on a headland that will be seen far out at sea. Such mounds on high places were not uncommon. There is a parallel with the pyre of Achilles and Patroklos in Homer's *Odyssey*, 24. Beowulf's underwater battles make a sea monument fitting

endelaf (last man): (l.2813) Wiglaf is now the last of the Waymundings as Beowulf is childless. He is also Beowulf's successor in spirit and heroism

sothfaestra dom (the glory of the righteous): (l.2820) many see this as a Christian statement implying that Beowulf goes to heaven. The Old English literally states 'the doom [fate] of those who are righteous' and there is no hint as to which code—pre-Christian heroic or Christian—Beowulf practises. The statement is deliberately ambiguous

---

Wiglaf reproaches the coward   lines 2821–2891

Wiglaf laments Beowulf's death, but his success means that the dragon will no longer have power over the treasure. No one could have withstood the dragon's poisonous blast. The cowards emerge from the wood and Wiglaf speaks sternly to them. He reminds them of Beowulf's gifts of armour to them. He then narrates the events of the battle, modestly playing down his own part. He predicts exile for the cowards and claims that death would have been better.

NOTES AND GLOSSARY:

Bona (The slayer): (l.2824) the dragon

homera lafe (the hammer's legacy): (l.2829) a kenning for a sword

hildlatan (battle-shirkers): (l.2846) the cowardly Geats who fled. There is an inconsistency here as Beowulf earlier requested to be left alone in this battle. But such a reproach would heighten the praise of Wiglaf

lines 2884–91: this harsh punishment implies exile and the cessation of all that the *comitatus* (see page 51) stands for. There are parallels here with Grendel as exiled wanderer. It has been suggested that Wiglaf is advising suicide to the cowards

---

The messenger's speech   lines 2892–3027

Wiglaf sends a messenger to the stronghold with the news. The messenger predicts attacks by Frisians and Franks. Hygelac's war against the Franks would be revived, now the Geats were weaker. The Swedes would probably attack as well. Ongentheow of Sweden had killed Hathkin at Ravenswood, but Hygelac had avenged that death, Eofor, Hygelac's son-in-law, having killed Ongentheow. It was not surprising therefore that a Swedish attack was imminent. The messenger suggests that they all go to the cave and bring Beowulf's body to the funeral pyre on which they will place treasure. The messenger predicts exile and terror for the Geats.

NOTES AND GLOSSARY:

Hugas: (1.2914) a Frankish tribe
Hetware: (1.2916) a Frankish tribe
Merewioingas (the Merovingian king): (1.2924) King of the Franks
Hrefnawudu: (1.2925) literally, 'Ravenswood'. This refers to the
                        first Swedish war. See Part 3, Commentary,
                        pp.68–9
Eofor and Wulf: (ll.2964–5) these Geatish brothers, sons of Wond-
                        red, kill Ongentheow and avenge King Hathkin's
                        death. Both sides are praised for their valour and
                        called by fine titles. Wulf, 'Wondred's brave son'
                        deals Ongentheow a great blow which is returned
                        by the Swedish king: both are badly wounded and
                        Eofor fatally wounds Ongentheow. Both brothers
                        survive to be rewarded by the new king, Hygelac,
                        'Hrethel's offspring'
sio faehtho (this feud): (1.2999) it is over fifty years since this feud
                        occurred and Beowulf was innocent of all aggres-
                        sion. But this shows the strength and importance
                        of the spirit of revenge. It is simply a credit to Beo-
                        wulf that he has kept peace so long
lines 3010–15:   the messenger talks of the treasure burned on the
                        pyre. In fact the treasure is buried later in the
                        mound. Only armour is on the pyre (ll.3119–40).
                        There is a mixture of pagan cremation ceremony
                        and possibly Christian mound burial
hleahtor alegde (laid aside his mirth): (1.3020) a euphemism for death
hrefn (raven):   (1.3024) a bird of prey conventionally mentioned in
                        Old English battle poetry, yet nowhere else do the
                        birds speak to each other

Beowulf's funeral   lines 3028–end

The Geats sorrowfully go to Earnaness and see Beowulf, the dead dragon and the treasure. God had permitted Beowulf alone to open the
treasure hoard. A curse had been laid on anyone who plundered the
hoard. Wiglaf recounts how he brought out the treasure and what Beowulf's wishes for a funeral were. He orders the pyre to be made and the
hero's body to be placed on it. Seven thanes carry the treasure from the
cave and push the dragon over the cliff.

Beowulf's body is placed amongst armour and the flames burn high.
Loud lamentation is heard and a Geatish woman sings a dirge in which
she fears future calamities for the Geats. A mound is raised high on the
cliff and visible as a beacon far out to sea. Treasure is placed in the

barrow with Beowulf's remains. Twelve warriors ride round the barrow singing a dirge in which they praise Beowulf's manliness, strength, mildness, kindness and his eagerness for fame.

NOTES AND GLOSSARY:

Earnanaes: (l.3031) literally, 'Eagles' ness', a promontory in Geatland

galdre bewunden (hedged about with a spell): (l.3052) the dragon's treasure has a magical spell attached to it, as is common in folk legend (for example, in the *Nibelungenlied*). The curse is given a Christian flavour by stating that God allowed a chosen one to touch it; ll.3069−73 underline this Christian aspect of the curse

lines 3074−5: all who plunder the gold will be damned, but Beowulf had not looked on it too eagerly. This implies that Beowulf's motives were good: he had taken the gold not for avaricious reasons but because of his quarrel with the gold-hoard's dragon

raed aenigne (any reason): (l.3080) it appears that Wiglaf tried to dissuade Beowulf from this exploit

thaes Waldendes waere (in the Ruler's keeping): (l.3109) Scyld Shefing also passes into 'God's keeping' on his death (l.27). This appears to be the Christian afterlife

on hlytme (by lot): (l.3126) there were many volunteers, so it was unnecessary to cast lots

lines 3137−48: Beowulf's funeral. See Part 3, Commentary, pages 76−8. The lament is common in both pagan and Christian funerals, for example, Hildeburh's lament (l.1117)

giomorgyd (the lament): (l.3150) it is common for a woman to sing a funeral lament, but it has been suggested that this might refer to Beowulf's widow, although no mention of a wife has been made in the poem. C.L. Wrenn hypothesises that it was Hygd, Hygelac's widow. Her elegy is more for herself and the Geats than for Beowulf

hlaew (stronghold): (l.3157) the text could be either *hlaew*, 'barrow', or *hleo*, 'shelter'; both would be feasible. It is primarily the sense of 'beacon' that is important, a sign and monument for others to see

gold on greote (gold in the dirt): (l.3167) the final irony is that the gold is returned to rot in the earth from whence it came

lofgeornost (keenest for fame): (l.3182) the final praise of Beowulf is ambiguously Christian and heroic: his physical strength, honour, love, gentleness and kindness, while the final 'keenest for fame' suggests the prime driving force of the heroic warrior—to achieve as great a reputation on earth as possible. C.L. Wrenn calls it 'a perfect blending of Christian and Germanic heroic statement' (see his edition of *Beowulf with the Finnesburg Fragment*, Harrap, London, 3rd edn, 1973, p.228)

Part 3

Commentary

Germanic society

The *comitatus*

Although *Beowulf* is set in Scandinavia, it is safe to talk about a code of behaviour and morality common to all Germanic races in the early Middle Ages. It also appears that the poet had his own society in mind as much as a sixth-century Scandinavian one. The most important concept, the binding force of society, was the *comitatus*, the mutual loyalty between lord and thane or warrior. The leader gave legal and economic protection (which included armour and gold) in return for military services. It is largely a personal relationship and cuts across tribes, as we see men of different races serving Hrothgar and Hygelac. Beowulf and Wiglaf are not Geats but Waymundings who owe allegiance to the Geatish king. Tacitus, the Roman soldier, senator and historian, explains this relationship in his work *Germania* (AD 98):

> As for leaving a battle alive after your chief has fallen, *that* means lifelong infamy and shame. To defend and protect him, to put down one's own acts of heroism to his credit—that is what they really mean by 'allegiance'. The chiefs fight for victory, the companions for their chief. Many noble youths . . . deliberately seek out other tribes where some war is afoot . . . you cannot maintain a large body of companions except by violence and war.*

We can see many of these points exemplified in *Beowulf*: Wiglaf sharply rebukes Beowulf's followers for retreating and not aiding their lord: 'Death is better / for any earl than an existence of disgrace' (ll.2890−1). We see how Beowulf plays down his heroic acts and praises Hrothgar and Hygelac instead; Wiglaf similarly underplays his part in the dragon fight: 'I was little equipped to act as a body-guard' (ll.2877−8), although he dealt the decisive blow.

The lord's part of the deal is often summed up by gift-giving. Wiglaf chastises the cowards for accepting treasure and armour and not fulfilling their part of the *comitatus* bargain. Beowulf has quite wasted these

---

* *Tacitus: On Britain and Germany*, trans. H. Mattingly, Penguin Books, Harmondsworth, 1948, p.112.

gifts, he states (ll.2864–72). The lord's or leader's function is made clear in his titles of *hring-fengel* 'ring-prince' (l. 2345), *gold-wine* 'gold-friend' or 'lord' (ll.1602, 1171, 1476), *gold-gyfa, sinc-gifa* 'gold-giver', 'treasure-giver' (ll.2652, 2311, 1342). Gold would have been kept in the shape of arm-bands which were easily transported and safely kept; the many references to rings and ring-giving allude to this practice. In the Old English *Maxims*, a poetic collection of wise sayings, we hear that 'King shall rule kingdom. . . . The king in hall / Must share out rings.'

The hall

The central location for the *comitatus* society was the hall, called the gift-hall, gold-hall or mead-hall in *Beowulf*. Heorot was such a place and it comes to represent the entire Danish society. Here vows of allegiance were interchanged, heroic boasts made, and feasting and mead-drinking carried out. Tacitus refers to the Germanic love of banqueting and entertainment, especially at ceremonial occasions, and we see Hrothgar conducting much of his business at a feast, while Queen Wealhtheow circulates with the cup. Great significance is given to protocol and seating arrangements, and it is here that promises of future aid are made. In the hall the poet narrates the legends of past glory and keeps the reputation of dead heroes alive, or he composes new songs out of his 'word-hoard' to celebrate recent victories. When the Christian poets wished to find an image for this world or for paradise, they chose the mead-hall, as this represented order, social concord and perfected life. The threat to Heorot by Grendel has far greater consequences than the collapse of a building; it refers to the civilisation itself. To call Grendel the new hall-thane implies that evil now has control in Denmark.

In spite of the order and peace in the hall, we are frequently shown the tensions that lie just beneath the surface. When Wealhtheow pleads for her sons' succession, when we are told of future feud and fire, we are aware how fragile this peace is. We have the perfect example in Ingeld's hall when old feuds can be fanned into fiery troubles as the feasting progresses. The brittleness and tension in the hall reflect the tenor of Germanic life as a whole. Beowulf is exceptional in his ability to keep peace in hall and country for a lifetime, but eventually his hall and kingdom are also destroyed.

Revenge

Each member of the *comitatus* was responsible for redressing any wrongs suffered by a kinsman or inflicted by him. Revenge had to be dealt out or a fixed amount of money or possessions given or received as a settlement. Tacitus states that a man has to take over the feuds as well as the loyalties of his kinsmen, and that murder can be compensated for by cattle, not necessarily blood revenge. This compensation for the death of a kinsman was called *wergild* or 'man-price', and the fixed amount would depend on the social status of the dead man. Hrothgar tells us how he paid the *wergild* that Beowulf's father Edgetheow owed after he had killed Heatholaf; Edgetheow was considered an exile, out of the *comitatus*, until this settlement was completed, and the Geats were presumably unable to meet this amount. We are told of the tragedy that Grendel causes as *wergild* cannot be paid by a monster: 'the blood-price was unpaid. / Nor did any counsellor have cause to look for / a bright man-price at the murderer's hand' (ll.154–8). *Beowulf* is full of tales of revenge—the Finn episode, the Ingeld tale, the Swedish Wars, Grendel's mother's revenge.

The ultimate tragedy occurs when accidental death happens. Hathkin unintentionally kills his brother Herebeald and Hrethel their father is unable to avenge the death in any way, as this is not possible for a relative:

A sin-fraught conflict that could not be settled,
unthinkable in the heart; yet thus it was,
and the atheling lost his life unavenged.

(ll.2441–3)

Vengeance, therefore, was a vital part of Germanic life, governed by strict laws and amounts of compensation, and the utmost humiliation was to leave a kinsman unavenged, as Hrethel was obliged to do.

Edgetheow was exiled from Geatland and Wiglaf predicts exile for the cowardly thanes who deserted Beowulf. An exile could be killed without *wergild* being paid and it was the worst possible existence conceivable. The plight of the exile is clearly illustrated in many Old English elegies and the later Old Icelandic sagas. Grendel and Cain are described in terms of the exile, the *angenga* 'solitary one' (l.165) who trod the tracks of exile (l.1352), Ohthere's sons Eanmund and Eadgils are exiles (*wraec-maecg*, l.2379) and it is significant that the coastguard can only conceive of two reasons why anyone should leave his hall: adventure or exile (l.338), and Beowulf does not look like an exile.

Reputation and glory

A well-known Old Norse verse from the *Hávamál* states that 'Possessions die and relations die, one also dies oneself; I know of one thing which never dies: the reputation surrounding every dead man.' The word for reputation here is *dómr*, Old English *dōm*, which gives us our modern English doom. But in Old English it means one's glory, reputation, fame (as well as other senses of judgement, opinion, will, sense); it is posterity's judgement of one's life, and for the pre-Christian hero it means his after-life. Reputation is often called 'the pagan consolation' of worldly fame. *Dom* is one of these Old English words with many meanings clustered around it, and it was adopted by the Christians to mean (Christian) glory. The *Hávamál* saying is echoed in the Old English *Maxims* where we learn that all shall depart, property be divided, but *dom bith selest*, 'fame is best'.

Beowulf exhorts Hrothgar not to mourn for Ashhere but, as 'each of us can expect an end to his worldly life; let him who is capable of doing so, gain *dom* before his death; that is the best thing for the departed warrior afterwards' (ll.1386–9). This is the highest sentiment and aim for the warrior and it is something that must continually be striven for; one cannot gain a fine reputation and then relax, for *dom* is the accumulated fame of one's entire life, the judgement of others on one's life. Wiglaf reminds Beowulf when he has had a setback in his dragon fight: 'Beloved Beowulf, accomplish all things well, as you declared long ago in the days of your youth, that you would not allow your *dom* to perish while you were still alive' (ll.2663–6).

Hygelac pays Beowulf the great compliment of saying that he is 'a man renowned for his combats and good deeds [who] conducted himself in pursuit of *dom*' (ll.2178–9). It may appear as if Beowulf is too conscious of his desire for glory, too calculating in his aspirations to perfection, but this is too modern an interpretation. He is simply *domgeorn*, 'eager for glory' as many heroes are called, and the final word the poet has about Beowulf is that he is *lofgeornost*, 'most eager for praise' (l.3182), a concept akin to fame. Hrothgar also ascribes to Beowulf eternal fame: 'You yourself have performed such deeds that your *dom* will live eternally' (ll.953–5). What more could be asked?

The opposite state is that of being *domleas*, 'deprived of glory', and such a one in *Beowulf* is Unferth who forfeited *dom* by his cowardly act (l.1470). Heremod also provides a bad example by not giving gifts *aefter dome* 'to obtain fame' (l.1720).

This desperate need to achieve glory and fame is one of the reasons for the high position of the *scop* or poet. In *Widsith* we hear that the poets always meet, south or north, someone who wishes to have his *dom*, 'fame', raised up before warriors. This patron will gain praise and has under the heavens *heahfaestne dom*, 'very secure fame'; in return the poet is rewarded with liberal gifts. This relationship is akin to that of the thane; the poet gives verbal support and aid to his lord's immortality by singing praises of the lord's exploits to which his other thanes have contributed.

Weird or Fate

The warrior cannot rely solely on his strength; there is also the super-natural to take into consideration. As with much of the thought in the poem, there is an intricate mingling of pagan and Christian ideas, and the concept of fate is no exception. Just as the Christians 'baptised' the heroic concept *dom*, 'fame', to include the Christian sense of heavenly glory, so also the idea of an amoral or at worst malignant fate that ruled men's lives was adapted to include the Christian sense of divine providence, God's benevolent and infinite plan for mankind. For this reason the poet's conception of fate sometimes appears contradictory. *Gaeth a wyrd swa hio scel*, 'Fate always takes its own course' (l.455), is Beowulf's own statement, as he acknowledges a power greater than his own strength. But we also hear that more men would have been killed by Grendel 'had not the God overseeing us, and the resolve of a man, / stood against this Weird' (ll.1056−7). The poet continues by reinforc-ing God's influence over fate: he guided the action then, as he does even now. Klaeber (p.170) states that this passage 'enjoins rational trust in the governance of the Almighty and readiness to accept what-ever may be in store for us, be it good or evil'. Significantly the word for God here is *Metod*, usually translated 'ruler', but it originally meant 'the measurer' or 'the ordainer of fate' in a pre-Christian context. *Wyrd* in this context is subject to God who is benevolent and willing to avert tragedy. In addition to God's help this quotation men-tions Beowulf's resolve or courage (*mod*), and this is substantiated by comments like *Wyrd oft nereth / unfaegne eorl, thonne his ellen deah*, 'Fate often saves the undoomed man if he is courageous' (ll.572−3). Here it looks as if man himself is responsible for his fate, though the catch is in the word 'undoomed' and can lead to a disturbing 'Fate often helps those not fated, if they are courageous'! A clearer comment on God's role and the influence of providence is seen in the following:

> But God was to grant to the Geat people
> the clue to war-success in the web of fate—
> His help and support. . . . The Almighty Lord
> has ruled the affairs of the race of men
> thus from the beginning.

(ll.696−702)

The web of fate conjures up images of the classical, pagan concept of the web of destiny, but here it is quite clear that God is superior in power and knowledge. It appears that the idea of any amoral, inexor-able fate coexists with that of benevolent, divine providence with no contradiction. In addition there is a strong sense of God helping those who help themselves. A clue is given in Hrothgar's 'sermon', although there is no mention here of fate as such. God gives men wisdom, dominion and strength—gifts which must be properly used, for at some time some worldly force, such as illness, old age or even death, will take them away. 'What change of fortune befell me', Hrothgar exclaims. No fault of his own, only *wyrd*, or the ways of this world, deprived him of his worldly gifts. This view of fate, rather akin to nature, can be controlled by courageously living a virtuous life according to the heroic code. The interaction between fate and providence does not appear to bother Beowulf or the poet and should not cause the reader any concern: Christian *wyrd* is simply a new variety of wine in an old bottle.

The major characters

Beowulf

There is some allusion to most of the characters in *Beowulf* in medieval chronicles or legends, and many we know existed. But there is no evidence of a man called Beowulf from Geatland ever having lived. His name does not appear in other legends as a folk-hero or dragon-slayer, as might have been thought, had he been so popular. The *Widsith* poet mentions Hrothgar, Hrothulf, Eormanric, Hnaef, Ongentheow, Offa, the Geats, Swedes and Danes, Eadgils and Eadwin and many more, but no Beowulf. C.L. Wrenn states: 'the historicity of Beowulf himself, then, must remain for the present as "not proven", but by no means impossible'.* We do have a tenth-century reference to a field named Beowa near Grendel's mere in England, but these names were probably inspired by the poem. It is likely that the hero's name is invented, but in many ways he reflects the traditional Germanic hero. His unpromising start to life, his king's doubts about him and discouragement, his sudden blossoming, heroic appearance, superhuman strength, dragon fighting, and his embodiment of all Germanic virtues, all point to the well-known hero of the north, found in sagas or other Germanic legends. He embodies all the virtues of the hero-warrior, being perfect in every respect.

He is both superman with the strength of thirty, and also very human, as he is aware that he is ruled by Weird, subject to fortune. He is proud as a hero should be but not arrogant; he makes the correct boasts about his intended success, and he carries them out successfully; he is offered the Geatish throne, but refuses it; he does all to achieve

---

* *Beowulf with the Finnesburg Fragment*, 3rd edn, 1973, p.45.

peace and only fights when peace is threatened, unlike Hygelac. He gives gifts, rules perfectly when a king, and is always courteous, eloquent, diplomatic and well-mannered. At his death he has no regrets:

> I have guarded this people
> for half a century; not a single ruler
> of all the nations neighbouring about
> has dared to affront me with his friends in war, . . .
>   In all of these things,
> sick with my life's wound, I may still rejoice:
> for when my life shall leave my body
> the Ruler of Men may not charge me
> with the slaughter of kinsmen.

(ll.2732—43)

As Wiglaf reminds Beowulf (ll.2663—8), he has done all things well and gained eternal glory, the aim of every warrior, and the necessary after-life of fame.

Such a portrait incorporates much more than expected of the Germanic hero, if he is compared with similar figures in Norse literature. He has compassion, love, gentleness, graciousness; and the four attributes the poet ascribes to him at the conclusion—gentlest, most gracious, kindest, keenest for fame—are not the most typical. In fact they might describe a Christian saint, if the fame were with God and not only fellow-man. Beowulf is also meticulous in his praise and thanks to God on all occasions. Klaeber states that 'the main story has been thoroughly imbued with the spirit of Christianity'. Another critic has described Beowulf as 'neither human nor superhuman, pagan nor Christian, English nor Geatish, heroic nor humble—but something of them all and more.' He is very much a literary character created to embody a principle or even a way of life. His actions make him exemplary, so that if the reader is left at the conclusion with a sense of futility or loss it is a reflection on this principle and its limitations. Possible confusion might come from the fact that the poet greatly admires this code, Germanic heroism, and is attracted by the courageous life it inspires in its adherents, but he also, as a Christian, seems aware of its limitations, and the ultimate futility of a life governed by fate and with no hope of the eternal joy of heaven. The poet continually stresses the brevity of the peace, joy and order that anyone can hope to achieve: Hrothgar will indeed precipitate feud by his marriage-bond peace treaty. At every point of celebration sorrow is predicted, or past tragedy remembered in a lay or memory. And after Beowulf's death we sense that 'the rest is silence'. Beowulf's after-life, in spite of many critics' comments about salvation, is highly ambiguous. He goes to seek *sothfaestra dom* (l.2820), 'the judgment of the righteous ones'; he receives the fate of the just, whatever that is. J.R.R. Tolkein sums up Beowulf's departure in this way:

> [Beowulf] thinks at the end only of his barrow and memorial among men, of his childlessness, and of Wiglaf, the sole survivor of his kindred, to whom he bequeathes his arms. His funeral is not Christian, and his reward is the recognized virtue of his kingship and the hopeless sorrow of his people.*

There is a tendency to see Beowulf as a saviour figure and some critics have stressed the parallels with Christ. He leads a band to conquer evil and descends into the evil waters to cleanse the world of monsters that are closely connected to primal evil. Such parallels must not be overstressed but simply add to the overall picture of the perfect hero who conquers the wicked and creates peace. Parallels might likewise be made with Arthur, who mysteriously arrives to save England and departs, like Scyld Shefing by boat. We are here in the realm of archetype and mythic associations which must be handled with care.

The character of Beowulf is rarely described by the poet. We see him by his actions and through others' eyes. Our first impression of him is from the coastguard who immediately sees that he has 'the head of a hero' (l.251); Hrothgar's chamberlain also recognises him as a great man. Unferth's slanderous attack on Beowulf's reputation gives Beowulf a chance to relate an earlier adventure, the Breca episode—a battle that proves his supernatural strength and courage and foreshadows his later matches with monsters. After this Beowulf's own actions speak for themselves. We see him as someone who acts, rather than contemplates. In the first part there is a strong contrast between Beowulf the energetic actor and Hrothgar the morose bystander: 'It is better for a man / to avenge his friend than to refresh his sorrow' (ll.1384–5), Beowulf encourages the Danish king.

It is therefore not surprising that when the dragon strikes in Geatland Beowulf immediately decides to attack. We are not meant to compare the attitudes of the two kings to their problems. Some have suggested that King Beowulf should not have endangered his life and thereby his country's prosperity by taking on the challenge single-handed. The duty of the king was different from that of a warrior and, as in chess, he should not expose himself to peril. Hrothgar was never criticised for waiting and perhaps Wiglaf would have come along as the new hero. Such speculation is not helpful; Beowulf is an actor, a challenger, a hero ever mindful of his reputation, and such a dramatic end is surely preferable for a man who is *lofgeornost*, 'most eager for praise', than the feebleness of old age.

* *'Beowulf*: the monsters and the critics', in Lewis E. Nicholson (ed.), *An Anthology of Beowulf Criticism*, University of Notre Dame Press, Notre Dame, Ind., 1963, pp.95–6.

Beowulf's strength or success diminishes as the matches proceed. Grendel's mother, we are told, is weaker than her son, but to defeat her Beowulf requires more effort and a magical sword, while he needs a helper to slay the dragon. Perhaps there is some relationship between the evil of the adversary and the ease with which it is defeated. Grendel had no excuse, his mother wished to avenge her son and the dragon was provoked by the slave.

Beowulf finally achieves his wish: his grave becomes a beacon for all to see. His life is an example for all to follow and he attains *ece dom*, 'eternal glory'.

Hrothgar

King Hrothgar of Denmark would probably have been known to the Anglo-Saxon audience. In the Old English poem *Widsith* (?seventh century) Hrothgar and his nephew Hrothulf are mentioned as defeating Ingeld of the Heathobards at Heorot. He was known in Latin chronicles as Ro and in Old Norse sagas as Hróarr, and is accredited with establishing a great royal seat at Roskilde ('Ro's fountain') in Zealand in Denmark. In Norse legend there is some confusion about Hrothgar and Hrothulf's relationship, but we can surmise from hints in this poem and *Widsith* that Hrothgar has had constant feuds with the Heathobard tribe, perhaps with Froda. Hrothgar wishes to cement a peace treaty by marrying his daughter Freawaru to Ingeld, Froda's son, but this attempt misfires and fresh feud breaks out, ending in the Heathobards' burning down Heorot (see ll.82–3). That the story of Ingeld was well known to the Anglo-Saxons is testified in a letter Alcuin wrote to the Bishop of Lindisfarne in 797; he criticises the monks' love of heroic legend rather than religious stories and asks 'What has Ingeld to do with Christ?' Finally Ingeld is defeated by Hrothgar and Hrothulf, information we glean from *Widsith*.

The poet deliberately gives an added dimension of historical fact to the tale. In addition, by assuming the audience's knowledge of Hrothulf's later treachery, Heorot's burning, and so on, the poet can add hints of tragic anticipation which flavour the tone of the whole poem (see ll.82–5 and 1014–19).

The character of Hrothgar as a wise and peace-loving king is also substantiated by the Lejre Chronicle (*c*.1770), Saxo Grammaticus's *Danish History* (*c*.1200) and sagas. The *Beowulf* poet develops this character outline into a great king who is generous and beloved, perhaps with the famous biblical patriarchs in mind. Apart from Beowulf's mild scepticism about Hrothgar's attempt to create peace by marriage, a scepticism that implies that Hrothgar naïvely underrates the Germanic need for vengeance, there is not a breath of criticism of Hrothgar in the entire poem. Beowulf immediately supposes that the dragon's wrath has been caused by his own fault ('The chieftain [Beowulf] supposed he had sorely angered / the Ruler of all', ll.2329–31), yet Hrothgar never considers the possibility that Grendel's wrath is caused by him or the Danes. He briefly outlines his career at the conclusion of his sermon (ll.1769–84): he ruled successfully for fifty years and defended his nation úntil there were no enemies. Then his luck changed, Grendel came and joy turned to grief. He takes the attacks as an act of bad fortune, just as Beowulf's success is good luck—aided by God.

There is implied and mild criticism of the Danes' attitude in many places and this might be taken as a reflection on the king. The Danes are passive and pessimistic, while Beowulf and the Geats are active and optimistic. A good example is when Beowulf is in Grendel's mere and a group of Geats and Danes watch at the surface (ll.1591–1605). The Danes are old, wise and experienced, and give up hope of Beowulf's return: 'the kindly gold-giver' (again no criticism, only praise) returns home, 'but the foreigners [the Geats] sat on in hope'. Naturally Beowulf returns against all odds and the jubilant, rejoicing Geats with Grendel's head on a spear boldly enter Heorot. Beowulf, 'a man who had dared deeds and was adorned with their glory,' leads what must have been a noisy and awesome band with the monster's head held high into the hall, where in contrast the despairing Danes are drinking. With typical understatement the poet states that the Danes 'eyed it well'. Such a contrast shows the Danes in an unfavourable light. Similarly when Beowulf rightly rebuffs Unferth's criticism he counter-attacks by suggesting that the Danes are all talk and no action: 'had your heart's intention / been so grim for battle as you give us to believe' (ll.593–4). Grendel 'expects no resistance' from the Danes (ll.600–2). The Danes collapse in despair and fall back on heathen practices (ll.171–88), while Beowulf invariably acts and thinks positively without being too proud. Fate, states Beowulf, *can* be changed if a man has courage. God aids those who aid themselves is the message that one gets, and the Danes are not keen on self-help. But such criticism is aimed at the Danes. There is the feeling that the king himself, as in a game of chess, should not endanger the entire nation by going to the battle front but should direct affairs and protect himself. (Such a concept has been used to criticise King Beowulf's single-handed battle with the dragon.)

Perhaps another suspicious note at Heorot is the way Hrothgar surrounds himself with doubtful counsellors. Unferth is seen to be a true 'peace-breaker', a murderer of his kin, a coward and slanderer, while Hrothulf we know will prove an arch-traitor. Wealhtheow seems more aware of the dangers of Hrothgar's naïvety, as she tempers his enthusiasm with words of warning.

We should not be too eager to find fault with Hrothgar when we are continually told of his greatness (although some say that these many compliments come too frequently and ring false). Wisdom and old age go together in Anglo-Saxon society and Hrothgar is no exception. It is significant that after Beowulf's triumphant entry into Heorot with Grendel's head, when the above-mentioned contrast between Danish passivity and Geatish action is clearly made, Hrothgar launches into his sermon which is in many ways a warning to Beowulf (see pp.69–71).

The female characters

The women we meet in *Beowulf*—Wealhtheow (Hrothgar's queen), Hygd and Freawaru (Hygelac's wife and daughter) and Hildeburh, the Danish princess in the Finn episode, all seem to be passive and keen to create peace amongst the warriors, while some suffer incredibly. We are told that the position of an Anglo-Saxon lady was much better than her post-Conquest counterpart: a wife was more independent, could hold land in her own right, could keep her 'bride price' and property and was given a 'morning-gift' the day after marriage; and on her death her property passed to her kinsmen, if she were childless, not to her husband. A widow could choose her next husband without undue pressure. In the *Maxims* of the Exeter Book we find the following prescription:

> A king has to procure a queen with a payment, with goblets and with rings. Both must be pre-eminently liberal with gifts ... the woman must excel as one cherished among her people, and be buoyant of mood, keep confidences, be open-heartedly generous with horses and with treasures; in deliberation over the mead, in the presence of the troop of companions, she must always and everywhere greet first the chief of those princes and instantly offer the chalice to her lord's hand, and she must know what is prudent for them both as rulers of the hall.*

Tacitus seems surprised by the high status of women and marital morality in Germanic society, especially by the fact that a man has only one wife and that the husband brings a dowry to the wife; he states:

> The German women live in a chastity that is impregnable, uncorrupted by the temptations of public shows or the excitement of banquets. They take one husband, like the one body or life that they possess. No thought or desire must stray beyond him. They must not love the husband so much as the married state.... Good morality is

* Translation by S.A.J. Bradley, *Anglo-Saxon Poetry*, Dent, London, 1982, p.348

more effective in Germany than good laws in some places that we know.*

We see in *Beowulf* how kinsmen look after their women even after marriage, for example, when Hildeburh is taken home to her people after the tragic loss of brother, son and husband.

Wealhtheow is presented as the perfect queen, in particular in the traditional role of 'peace-weaver'. She passes the cup at feasts in correct order of precedence, moves amongst the warriors, old and young, and praises Beowulf, the guest of honour, before taking her place beside her husband. She is a model of diplomacy and tact as she subtly tries to ensure that her young sons succeed her husband and reminds Hrothulf, who presents a threat to the boys, of his obligations. As the audience would have known of Hrothulf's future treachery, Wealhtheow's efforts appear pathetic. Her major functions include being liberal with gifts, that is sharing her husband's duty as 'gift-giver', being the hostess at feasting and the creator of peace—functions which are all interconnected.

Queen Hygd of Geatland is also seen as fulfilling these duties. She is praised by comparing her with the cruel Thryth, Offa's queen, who made conflict and caused the deaths of her own men. This digression (ll.1931–62) would have a common, legendary source, akin to 'the taming of the shrew'. Hygd is also described as a great 'gift-giver' (ll.1929–31), and she seems to exercise a lot of authority, as it is she who offers Beowulf the Geatish throne on Hygelac's death, even when she has a son. We hear no more of her fate, but some critics have speculated that she is the Geatish woman who mourns at Beowulf's funeral, implying that Beowulf married Hygd; but there is no evidence for this.

The tragic and helpless situation of women is brought out in the Finn episode which concentrates on the plight of Hildeburh. This Danish princess is used as a pawn in the game of peace-making when she is married to King Finn of the Frisians, the traditional enemies of the Danes: 'guiltless she had suffered' the death of brother, son and husband. When the experiment in peace-weaving fails, she is returned to her own people. Hers is a life of sacrifice and mourning and she is treated most sympathetically by the poet, for example in the scene when she sings a lament at the funeral of her brother and son (ll.1117–18). She gives orders that her son should be cremated along with her brother, although the son would have been heir to the Frisian throne. The fragility of contracts aimed at achieving peace is emphasised by the concentration on Hildeburh and, by placing the episode directly after Wealhtheow's speech in which she attempts to weave peace, the poet stresses the hopelessness of Wealhtheow's mission and

* *Tacitus: On Britain and Germany*, trans. H. Mattingly, pp.116–17.

the vulnerability of women, and creates a mood of impending doom. This mood is strengthened by placing a scene of violent bloodshed beside one of joy and tranquillity in Heorot.

The poet employs a similar technique later. When Hygelac and Hygd are listening to Beowulf's tale of victory, the tragic tale of another woman used in the game of peace-making is inserted. We are told that Hrothgar's daughter, Freawaru, who was never mentioned when Beowulf was in Denmark, is betrothed to Ingeld, prince of the Heathobards, enemies of the Danes. Freawaru is an exemplary peace-weaver, we hear, and Beowulf surprisingly criticises Hrothgar for marrying her to Ingeld. He conjures up a scene that is more a prediction than fantasy: she will be brought home to Ingeld's hall and a Danish warrior accompanying her will be wearing trophies won from Heathobards in past feuds; trouble will ensue, old vengeances will be carried out and blood will flow. This will cause Ingeld's love for his wife to cool. This is the only note of criticism Beowulf ever makes about Hrothgar; he is strongly suspicious of the wisdom of peace by marriage. Edward Irving points out* that the bride is a thing, a passive object, whereas the sword is half-personified: 'it is seldom the slaying-spear sleeps for long —/seldom indeed—dear though the bride may be' (ll.2030−1). More slaughter occurs instead of peace, as the code they live by is based on the sword.

Apart from the above we hear of few women in *Beowulf*. We do not know if Beowulf had a wife, we only know he had no heir; we are not told the name of Beowulf's mother, while his father who was not even a Geat is often mentioned. Hygelac has a daughter who is nameless, but who is given to Eofor as a reward for killing the Swedish king, Ongentheow. Even the female monster remains as 'Grendel's mother'. Perhaps Anglo-Saxon women had many more privileges than Norman women, but we hear of few of them here. Their role is one of passively waiting and attempting to weave some peace in a hostile world.

The monsters

We have no clear picture of Grendel and his mother and no two readers would describe them alike. Did the poet expect us to know what they looked like from other legends, or did he deliberately wish us to use our imaginations? Today some critics have gone so far as to suggest that the monsters represent death, disease or war, symbols of the unforeseeable, undeserved calamities that strike. But the fact remains that the Anglo-Saxon audience would have believed in such monsters and seen them as wholly evil. John Gardner has written a fascinating novel

* *A Reading of Beowulf*, Yale University Press, New Haven, Conn., 1968, p.175.

called *Grendel* in which we see life from the monster's viewpoint and sympathise with the ugly, exiled creature, but no such sympathy could be expected in the Middle Ages. They belong to the group of wicked giants, demons (*thyrs, eoten*, 'giant').

What actual information do we have about them? At times they seem to be human: no creature yields a knife, as Grendel's mother does. Grendel has a glove or pouch for his victims; he is said to be related to Cain and therefore a son of Adam; he is called 'man' (*guma* and *maga*) and a 'hall-thane' who rules Heorot, though this could be ironically meant. Elsewhere it is said that he is 'in the shape of a man' and this parody of humanity is also seen in the fact that he has a soul which will go to hell (l.852). Later Beowulf states that Grendel will be judged at Doomsday (l.978), a fate reserved only for human souls.

The evil nature of the monsters is continually stressed. Grendel is *synnum beswenced*, 'afflicted with sins'; he is a *manscatha, synscatha*, 'evil doer'; *godes ansaca*, 'God's adversary'; *wonsaeli*, 'damned'; he is *haethen*, 'heathen' and *feond on helle*, 'enemy in hell'; and both monsters are called devils (l.1680) and the other epithets usually given to Satan (for example, *wergan gastes*, 'evil spirit').

Grendel's mother is also described in both human and demonic terms: she is *idese onlicnes*, 'shaped like a woman', *wif*, 'woman', and yet *brimwylf*, 'she-wolf of the sea' and *grund-wyrgen*, 'accursed monster of the deep'.

A key to the nature of Grendel and his mother lies in their being 'of Cain's kin'. Cain in Genesis was the unrepentant brother-murderer and in medieval tradition he represented the depths of evil after the Fall and before the cleansing Flood. He became a type of Wandering Jew, never to find peace or repentance, an evil outcast of society—half man, half devil. Cain and Grendel live in that twilight land of demonic, partially human creatures that later manifested themselves as werewolves (literally 'man-wolves'). Grendel is continually connected with night, darkness, and the farthest reaches from civilisation. He appears cannibalistic as he devours the Danish thanes.

If we are not told much about Grendel's physical appearance, his haunts are well described. He is a *mearcstapa*, one who wanders in the border region, an exile; he is *atol angengea*, 'a terrifying solitary one'. He lives in a place reminiscent of hell, and in fact the poet may have borrowed the description of Grendel's mere from a popular vision of hell. It is a cave under or behind a lake, a treacherous, windy, dark, frosty place yet with eerie fire on the water at night. The lake is infested with evil sea serpents and monsters and the water is fathomless and bloody. Instinctively the gentle hart would rather die than cross that water. In the *Maxims* we learn that 'Monster shall live alone on land among the fen.'

Abstract expressions such as *deathscua*, 'death shadow', 'bringer of chaos', 'denier of life', 'evil soul' surround Grendel. He is, in short, all that is diametrically opposed to Beowulf and to ordered society. The image that emerges is not of a tangible being but of an evil force. The first time he is mentioned directly follows the poet's song of Creation in the light and beautiful Heorot; in spirit with this song, the hall represents order, light, regeneration and life itself. It is a place of refuge, joy, peace and order and therefore hated by Grendel.

By being superhumanly strong Grendel makes an excellent opponent for Beowulf. By defeating a monster rather than a man Beowulf is raised above the ranks of ordinary hero and becomes a legendary superman. Yet both monsters and heroes are shown to be subject to fate and this also stresses the human aspect of Grendel.

Grendel is presented as the most evil of the monsters without a single redeeming feature, while the other two 'supernatural' beings have some slight cause for their anger. Grendel hates the 'daily beauty' of Heorot, while his mother, we are frequently told, follows the natural need to seek revenge; she has been quiet until her boy has been killed and now it is her duty to avenge his murder. The dragon who has behaved himself for three hundred years only turns aggressive when robbed and provoked.

The dragon, like Grendel, is a night creature who inhabits a distant cave in a wilderness and ravages the mead-hall in nocturnal raids. There is no doubt as to the nature of this creature. He is the well-known fire-breathing, gold-guarding, thick-skinned dragon that we find in folklore. In the *Maxims* we hear that 'the dragon must live in mound, old, proud in his ornaments'. Like Grendel the dragon is called *aeglaeca*, 'monster' (a word that comes to mean 'ugly', as outer appearances and inner character were thought to be closely connected); he is *theodsceatha*, 'foe of the people', *nythdraca*, 'hostile dragon', *guthsceatha*, 'destroyer'. But we are not told if he has a soul or not, and there are no terms that link him with the devil or absolute evil. We simply hear that his death was violent but do not know if hell awaited him. His body is pushed over the cliff into the seas, covered by water, like the monsters and giants of Genesis.

In spite of allusions to the devil and abstract concepts of evil, the monsters are very tangible creatures in *Beowulf*. They have no supernatural tricks, other than exceptional strength, and they are vulnerable and mortal. The early medieval audience would have accepted these monsters as monsters, not as symbols of plague or war, for such creatures were a definite reality.

Hygelac

The king of the Geats is also a historical character. We hear of him (as Chlochilaichus) in Gregory of Tours' *History of the Franks* (late sixth century) as the attacker of the kingdom of Theudoric, King of the Franks, who later sent his son to defeat Hygelac and his men. This raid must have occurred around AD 521. There is some confusion as to whether Hygelac is Danish or Geatish in the early accounts; this is probably due to a general lack of knowledge about Scandinavia, but the *Widsith* poet clearly differentiates between Swedes, Geats and South-Danes.

This fatal battle with the Franks is specifically referred to in *Beowulf*, first in connection with Wealhtheow's gift of a necklace which Hygelac was to wear when 'he provoked disaster / in the Frisian field' (ll.1206–7). Here we learn that his body and the necklace were carried off by the Franks. Later in a flashback when Beowulf prepares to fight the dragon, we hear again about Hygelac's fatal battle, but without any criticism this time: here he is 'that kindly lord of peoples, the king of the Geats' (ll.2354–9). We learn that Beowulf swam home, one of the few survivors, and that later he killed Dayraven (ll.2501ff.), the champion of the Franks and the man who killed Hygelac. Finally the messenger, after Beowulf's death, tells the Geats of the danger of fresh Frankish raids by reminding them of Hygelac's ill-fated mission. From a historical point of view, Hygelac is known as the king who provoked the Frankish wars. This is also the major memory of him in *Beowulf* after his death.

In the poem, however, we find King Hygelac described as the perfect gift-giving, beloved monarch. The description of his hall and court echoes that of Hrothgar and Heorot, although the former is much shorter: 'That was a handsome hall there. And high within it sat / a king of great courage' (ll.1925–6); 'the warlike young king, was well-known for his / giving of neck-rings' (ll.1969–70). Beowulf presents Hrothgar's treasure to Hygelac who in turn bestows the treasure of Hrethel on his nephew (the Geats' greatest treasure), and Hygelac gives him in addition an estate and a hall and makes him a chieftain. This exchange was expected of a victorious thane and grateful king for whom the thane had been fighting. Beowulf's glory enhances the king's reputation: 'to your people, O my prince [Hygelac], my performance there / will bring honour' (ll.2095–6), states Beowulf, and later claims that he fought 'in your name, Hygelac' (l.2131). This idea is expressed in Beowulf's compliment to Hygelac as he hands over Hrothgar's gifts:

> now, O bravest of kings, I bring them to you.
> I rejoice to present them. Joy for me, always
> lies in your gift.

(ll.2148–51)

At no point is there a strained relationship between the famous thane and the king as there is between uncle and nephew in the Danish court (Hrothgar and Hrothulf). Beowulf represents no threat:

> A kinsman knits no nets of malice
> darkly for his fellow. Does he devise the end
> of the man that is next to him? The nephew of Hygelac
> held fast to that man hardy in battle;
> each thought only of the other's welfare.
>
> (ll.2166–71)

In addition to Hygelac's involvement in the Frankish wars he is involved in the Swedish battles. The intricacies of these wars are unravelled elsewhere (pp.68–9). Hygelac is not the instigator but he takes over kingship and the feud from his brother Hathkin. Beowulf now fights for Hygelac and delights in repaying his uncle for his generosity. Eofor and Wulf also appear as champions, killing King Ongentheow of Sweden. In gratitude Eofor is given Hygelac's only daughter.

Much less is known of the Geats than of the Danes. We have historical references to them, apart from in *Widsith*, and it is generally held that they are the Gautar of Old Norse who inhabited the southern part of Sweden, Götland. This would make them the near neighbours of the Swedes to the north and close to Zealand and the Danes to the west. It might well be that the *Beowulf* poet made Beowulf a member of a less well known race to distance his legend of fantastic events, or it may be that the Geats were well known and that we hear nothing of them in historical records after the sixth century precisely because the tribe was annihilated, as the messenger predicts.

Wiglaf

We have no historical evidence of Wiglaf or his father Weoxstan. Wiglaf means 'battle remnant' and this is his major function. He is introduced at the conclusion of the poem as the sole survivor, the one true man who continues Beowulf's principles after the hero's death. At the end Beowulf adopts him as his heir and gives him the responsibility of attending 'to the people's needs henceforth'.

Weoxstan, Wiglaf and Beowulf are of the same small tribe, the Waymundings, probably originating in the border land between Geats and Swedes and bound to pay allegiance to one of their neighbours. Beowulf's father, Edgetheow, was attached to the Geatish royal house when he married Hrethel's daughter (Hygelac's sister), so that Beowulf was half-Waymunding, half-Geat. Weoxstan must have chosen the other side and been well considered in the Swedish court. Even at Beowulf's death Wiglaf is called a Scylfing (Swedish) prince.

Weoxstan aided Onela of Sweden in his contest for the Swedish throne against his nephews Eadgils and Eanmund, whom the Geats supported. Weoxstan even killed Eanmund and was greatly rewarded by Onela. However, when Eadgils became king he would have had to leave Sweden. In spite of Beowulf's active support of Eadgils, Weoxstan appears to have been well received by Beowulf, probably because of their common origins. Beowulf later bestowed on Wiglaf 'the wealthy dwelling-place of the Waymundings / confirming him in the landrights his father had held' (ll.2606–8). Onela had given Weoxstan his nephew Eanmund's armour, and this passes to Wiglaf on Weoxstan's death. It is therefore Eanmund's sword that Wiglaf uses to kill the dragon.

Wiglaf's courageous action is set in sharp contrast to the cowardly action of the other thanes. It becomes clear that the poet, who earlier had said Beowulf insisted on fighting alone, wishes to raise Wiglaf to the heights of folk hero. He becomes Beowulf's heir in more than the obvious sense in that he inherits all the virtues and principles that Beowulf embodied: loyalty to one's lord, courage, strength, graciousness and courtesy and the important eagerness for fame. Wiglaf provides a spark of hope in the otherwise bleak future for the Geats and indeed for the heroic ideal.

Significant themes and episodes

The Swedish Wars

The complex events surrounding the conflicts between Geatland and its northerly neighbour, Sweden, are narrated in brief, unchronological flashbacks while we anxiously await Beowulf's final and fatal combat. At the end of the poem we are told that the Geats can expect another crushing attack from Sweden which may totally annihilate the tribe. In the poem the second Swedish war is described before the first and the ballad-like flashback technique assumes some background knowledge.

Here are the events in chronological order. When King Hrethel of Geatland died (out of grief at his son Herebeald's accidental death) the Swedes take advantage of a weakened Geatland and ambush the Geats at Hreosnabeorgh (ll.2472–8). King Hathkin becomes king of Geatland after Hrethel and he leads an expedition into Sweden and captures Ongentheow's queen. Ongentheow quickly retaliates and rescues his queen, kills Hathkin and forces the Geats to take shelter in Ravenswood. The poet implies that it was the rash attack provoked by Hathkin that causes this disaster. Ongentheow showers the Geats all night long with threats of annihilation in the morning, but at dawn Hygelac, Hathkin's brother, emerges as a great warrior and drives the Swedes back. Ongentheow is cornered by two brave Geats, Eofor and his brother Wulf. There is a hard fight in which Wulf is badly wounded and Ongentheow killed. Both the Swedish king and the Geatish warriors are praised as courageous fighters. Hygelac is now king of the Geats and he richly rewards Eofor and Wulf, the former receiving Hygelac's daughter in marriage.

The fierce battle at Ravenswood appears to have settled the Swedish-Geatish feud, but only because of the strength of Hygelac and, presumably, Beowulf. Hygelac then loses his life in the ill-fated Frankish expedition and Beowulf escapes because of his swimming skill. Beowulf refuses the Geatish throne and supports Hygelac's son Heardred during his minority. Ohthere becomes king of the Swedes after Ongentheow but on his death the throne is seized by Onela, Ohthere's brother, while Ohthere's sons, Eanmund and Eadgils, seek help from Heardred when they have to flee from Sweden. Onela, however, leads a punitive expedition against his nephews and Heardred because of the help the latter had given. When Wiglaf and his ancestry are presented we hear that it was Weoxstan, Wiglaf's father, a Waymunding in the service of Onela, who killed Eanmund in that raid. On Heardred's death Beowulf becomes king of Geatland, and we learn that he gives support to Eadgils who leads a force against Onela, kills him and becomes king of Sweden.

The Geatish-Swedish wars create the backcloth to the events in the second part of the poem. Pieces in the mosaic of events are scattered throughout this section and help to create the mood of impending disaster. It is a story of continual attack and retaliation, stopped only during the strong reigns of Hrethel, Hygelac and Beowulf. Neither side has the better cause: Hathkin wants revenge, Ongentheow wishes his aged wife returned, Eofor protects his brother, Heardred aids fugitives, and Beowulf helps to depose a usurper. Both sides are described in laudatory terms, as both follow the heroic code that demands revenge. The wars, therefore, underline the theme that in a heroic society feuds can only temporarily be kept at bay and only by strong heroes. Like the monsters, war is bound to come again.

Hrothgar's 'sermon'

Beowulf returns to Heorot victorious after the fight with Grendel's mother and with the head of Grendel on a spear; he bursts into the hall where the Danes are drinking, having given up hope of Beowulf's success, and triumphantly announces that all the monsters are now dead: 'I avenged the violent slaughter / and outrages against the Danes'; now Heorot is 'free from care' as peace and order is restored. He then hands over the golden hilt of the giant sword with which he had killed the monster the blade of which had melted after the deed, leaving the engraved hilt.

Hrothgar meditates over the hilt before he launches into his long speech, sometimes called Hrothgar's sermon. The sword had belonged to the giants that lived before the Flood which had cleansed the world of these evil creatures (see also ll.111−14). Engraved on the hilt was the story of the original strife, the beginning of evil which was washed away by the Flood. Now its punitive part, the blade, had melted and the treasure part remained, now transferred from another evil creature, Grendel's mother, to Beowulf and later presented to the King of Denmark. The shift in ownership reflects the shift of power in Denmark away from the evil 'hall-thanes', the monsters, and back once more to Hrothgar and order.

This important introduction, far from being out of place, sets the tone and prepares for the moral of Hrothgar's sermon which is a warning about this worldly phenomenon of change from joy to woe and back to joy. It is also about how to administer one's gifts properly, both treasure and personal talents, and to guard against the inevitable onslaught of tragedy.

We can only guess what Hrothgar thinks while looking at the hilt. E.B. Irving suggests that it is 'the sudden and extreme shift of power'*.

The sermon itself is in three parts. Hrothgar begins by praising Beowulf for his heroism, modesty and wisdom, especially in the way he bears his 'great strength peaceably'. We must remember that, although the sermon is aimed at Beowulf, there is not the slightest note of censure of him. It is simply advice from the Danish 'shepherd from of old' to the young, inexperienced hero. Once more he praises Beowulf by contrasting him with the mean Heremod (see ll.898−915); God had given Heremod gifts of strength and position, but Heremod had not given rings, became cruel and was finally exiled. Beowulf, Hrothgar concludes, should learn from this the importance of generosity.

In the second part of the discourse Hrothgar discusses God's Providence: God gives power, wisdom and land to (noble)men and all goes well for a time. Then the prosperous man becomes complacent, proud and lazy; he does not *use* the gifts properly. Pride in early medieval thought was the worst sin possible, the sin of Lucifer, and it struck at the roots of the hierarchical society. God, like a Germanic ruler, gives out gifts to his 'thanes', wordly kings who in turn are expected to be generous. The imagery in this section echoes that of the New Testament, especially Ephesians 6:13−17 where faith is symbolised as armour. Hrothgar warns Beowulf about the 'chinks' of sin through which the arrows of Satan, 'the slayer' and 'the accursed one' will penetrate.

* *A Reading of Beowulf*, p.147. Irving's section on the sermon, pp.145−53, is excellent.

The theme of man's complacency, his selfish acceptance of all the world's gifts without thinking of the Giver or his fellow man, is very common in Old English verse; it is the ruling theme in the Junius Manuscript poems where the reversal of fortune is seen as a microcosmic Fall of Man. Grendel surely had thought himself ruler, and now he is defeated, like the evil giants in the Flood.

This leads Hrothgar into another favourite theme of the Church Fathers and in medieval literature in general, namely the contemplation of the brevity of life. Something must terminate man's joy at some point—sickness, the sword, flame, flood, a knife-stab, old age, blindness; or, if you are lucky, it need not be until death at an old age. But joy is worldly and cannot be for ever, and another will take over power and treasure. This theme is closely related to that of the use of treasure (see pp.72–4). Man with his freedom of will must *choose* to use God's gifts properly.

The third part of the sermon is about Hrothgar himself as an object lesson. He reigned for fifty years until he had no enemies, then a sudden and tragic change of fortune occurred in the shape of Grendel. Joy turned to sorrow. But again fortune has turned her wheel and joy has returned, and the sermon ends with Hrothgar brushing away the serious mood he has created, offering Beowulf treasure and inviting him to a feast.

His message is clear and well-timed. You are at the height of your fame now, Beowulf: you have youth, strength, success and many more gifts. I am not criticising you, but always be aware that a reversal can come through no fault of your own. Something must bring your success to an end, even if it is old age and death. Use your gifts as God distributes gifts to his thanes on earth and remember they are only temporary.

The message is found in much Old English poetry, and although Christian images are used here, the message is once more common to Christian and heroic codes. There is no mention of the major Christian consolation that eternal life is in store for the faithful and joy in heaven is for ever; there is no sense that this life is a temporary testing place, a valley of tears to be endured. We feel that life circumscribed by birth and death is *all*; nothing else is.

An old and wise man who has experienced much joy and sorrow, and who has recently suffered greatly, makes a heartfelt plea to a young man of extreme promise to recognise a major paradox in life. The speech also prepares us for the second part of the poem, as Beowulf is also to reign for fifty years in prosperity before trouble strikes.

The theme of gold and treasure

Tacitus in his *Germania* tells us that the warriors are

> prodigal in their demands on the generosity of their chiefs. It is
> always 'Give me that war-horse' or 'Give me that bloody and victor-
> ious spear'. . . . Such open-handedness must have war and plunder
> to feed it. . . . The chiefs take peculiar pleasure in gifts from neigh-
> bouring states . . . choice horses, splendid arms, metal discs,
> collars.*

Such a statement helps us to understand the importance placed on des-
criptions of the value and history of treasure and armour in *Beowulf*.
The poet seems to dwell, unduly for us today perhaps, on the gifts
Hrothgar gave Beowulf or the past history of the dragon's hoard. But
gold, treasure and armour play a vital part in the Germanic society. We
have already seen how the king is called 'gold-giver' or 'ring-giver'
(p.52) and the hall a 'gold-hall' or 'ring-hall', as if the distribution of
gold was the greatest function of the king. The poet equates liberality
with success as a ruler: give liberally when young, so that in old age you
have firm friends (ll.20–24), while the wicked king Heremod gave no
rings and dwelt an outcast. 'Learn from this, Beowulf', Hrothgar
stresses, 'study openhandedness!' (ll.1719–23).

God is also seen as a gift-giver, dispensing the treasures of this world
such as wisdom, lordship, leadership and prosperity, and it is the
king's duty to emulate God's bounty. If he fails then another king will
take his place (see Hrothgar's Sermon, ll.1724–68). The distribution
of gold, therefore, is the sign of the lord's faithfulness to his part of the
basic bargain between lord and thane. When Wiglaf criticises the
cowardly thanes he deliberately reminds them of the treasure they
received and how they have not kept their part of the bargain. 'Now
there shall cease for your race the receiving of treasure', Wiglaf predicts (lines 2884–6), and by this image he implies a total breakdown of
their social system, exile and death.

When Beowulf returns to Geatland he hands over the treasure he
received from Hrothgar to his king Hygelac (ll.2148–51), just as Wulf
and Eofor hand over King Ongentheow's armour to Hygelac (ll.2985–
90). The thane should play down his own triumphs and ascribe them to
his king, and also hand over all booty. In return, Beowulf, Wulf and
Eofor are generously repaid by Hygelac with treasure, land and, in the
case of Eofor, Hygelac's daughter. Beowulf in the Swedish wars fights
'to make return to Hygelac for the treasures he had given me' (ll.2490–3)
and he kills Dayraven the Frank who had slain Hygelac, so that

* *Tacitus: On Britain and Germany*, trans. H. Mattingly, pp.112–13.

Dayraven could not take Hygelac's armour back to *his* lord (ll.2503–4). As Tacitus states above, war is necessary both for booty to replenish the coffers from which the restless warriors are paid and to keep them occupied. It is here that the *Beowulf* poet's praise of peace and being free of war strikes us as being influenced by later Christian morality. But we are not to ask ourselves how King Beowulf solved the problem of war-hungry followers in his fifty years of peaceful reign nor to suppose that this was the cause of cowardly followers.

Gold, then, has to circulate; it has a *function* to perform or the society that possesses it will perish. Heorot ceases to function as a gold-hall when Grendel rules, implying that the Danish society collapses; it is significant that Grendel does not approach the treasure throne (ll.168–9), as he is outside this social order. Gold is useless to him, as it is to the dragon. The fate of treasure is therefore closely linked to the fortune of the tribe and for that reason we are told the past history and future fate of treasure. The gold in the dragon's hoard once belonged to a famous and wealthy race but both gold and tribe suffer the same fate of oblivion: they are 'death-rapt', and the treasure is buried in a barrow. Ironically it becomes Beowulf's property and sees the light of day for a very brief period, becoming buried again along with the king at the end. It is again out of circulation and its fate now symbolises the predicted fate of the lordless Geats:

> They left the earls' wealth in the earth's keeping,
> the gold in the dirt. It dwells there yet,
> of no more use to men than in ages before.

(ll.3166–8)

The story of a piece of jewelry appears unnecessary, but the poet subtly connects its fortune with its owners to give sinister and ironic hints of future disaster. Wealhtheow, for example, asking Beowulf to protect her sons in the future, gives Beowulf a priceless torque or necklace. It is immediately compared in value with the costly Brising necklace, and the poet reminds his audience (for the tale would have been well known) that the Brising necklace was stolen by Hama from the treacherous Eormenric. Secondly we are given a glimpse into the future when Hygelac wears the torque when 'in his superb pride he provoked disaster' in a Frisian feud (ll.1202–14). The torque, given by Beowulf to his queen (ll.2172–3), is passed to Hygelac who loses it and his life in a rash feud. Treachery seems to follow the necklace and therefore we might well query the outcome of Wealhtheow's fears as she uses it to buy protection for her sons. The audience would have known from other legends that they too were fated and that Hrothulf could turn treacherous. The poet's apparent digressions therefore play a vital role in creating suspense and subtly hinting at future events.

The same literary device is used when the poet describes armour and, in particular, swords. It is the sight of a sword heirloom that sparks off the Ingeld tragedy. Swords are equated with ancient treasure and their power and luck in battle follow them. We hear of the names given to swords in *Beowulf*—Hrunting or Nailing—and the giant sword plays a significant part not only in the battle with Grendel's mother but also in stressing the transience of races and power. Swords continue—this one from Creation even—and they are in themselves amoral, neither good nor bad. The giant sword's hilt is an object of great beauty, but belonged to giants and latterly Grendel's kin. The blade melts after Beowulf has used it to overthrow evil forces and in this way it shares the fate of its owners, but the hilt survives—a sign of passing ownership, thence of the mortality of man and the brevity of the time he can enjoy the things of this world. It is a fitting introduction to Hrothgar's Sermon.

Sutton Hoo and *Beowulf*

The Sutton Hoo archaeological find in Suffolk was uncovered in 1939. Under one of the mounds a 27-metre long ship was discovered with no body in it but much treasure, although in all respects it was a burial ship. The coins discovered on the site helped to date it at about AD 650, a period between the events mentioned in the poem and its composition. The discovery of this ship confirmed the account of Scyld Shefing's funeral found in *Beowulf* (ll.26−52), although Scyld's boat was pushed out to sea, not buried. The information gathered from the dig beautifully complements many points in the poem, which in turn can explain the significance of many items in the find. As in the Sutton Hoo ship Scyld is accompanied by treasure and armour, which includes a *signum* or standard and treasure 'from far countries'. The Sutton Hoo find includes a Coptic bowl from Alexandria, Byzantine spoons with Greek names of Saul and Paul which imply Christian origin, Celtic hanging bowls and possibly Swedish weapons. Amongst the treasure are a lute, a stag-tipped standard, a purse lid of great beauty, a large gold buckle as well as a helmet, sword and shield. A visit to this collection in the British Museum, London, is warmly recommended to appreciate the splendour of Anglo-Saxon art and the significance of the find.

Only a few points about the significance of the treasure can be made here. The first is the mixture of Christian and pagan artefacts. The bowls with crosses and the spoons with Saul and Paul (possibly christening presents) are definitely Christian, yet the idea of a ship burial is pagan, usually connected with the Germanic cult of Woden, as might be the zoomorphic shapes on the shield and the purse lid. We might say that a pagan king had objects of Christian origin in his treasure, taken from a booty or given by merchants. At any rate this mixture creates the same fascinating ambivalence about the intermingling of Christian and pagan elements as we find in *Beowulf*. Beowulf talks much of God and embodies many Christian virtues, yet his funeral is definitely pagan and his prime virtue of being most eager for fame is hardly the highest aim of the Christian. This interweaving of Christian and pre-Christian motifs and ideas is also seen in another Anglo-Saxon artefact, the Frank's Casket (late seventh century), on which scenes from heroic mythology (Weland the Smith, see *Beowulf*, l.455) and Christian narrative (the Adoration of the Magi) freely mingle without being out of place. This is a time of gradual conversion to Christianity, when enlightened missionaries used much of the existing religion and indeed many of the pagan temples. They adapted the early myths and code, stressing what was common to both.

The presence of a lute (which has now been reconstructed from fragments) among a great king's treasure confirms the importance of poetry and song in the Germanic hall. It also gives us an idea of the shape and sound of the Anglo-Saxon instrument that probably accompanied *Beowulf*. We know from another Old English poem, Caedmon's 'Hymn' that it was the custom to pass the harp or lute around as each member of the company recited a poem. In *Beowulf* we hear 'there was the music of the harp, / the clear song of the poet' (ll.89–90).

Another interesting point is the age of some of the objects in the find. The shield and the helmet were already over a hundred years old when placed in the mound, and this complements the many occasions in *Beowulf* when armour is called ancient heirlooms (for example ll.454, 1458, 2611, 2628). Great value was placed on the past history of armour to the point that swords are personified, given names and almost become warriors themselves.

The exquisitely interwoven designs on the jewelry and the intricate techniques used help us to understand some of the poet's techniques too. *Beowulf* is built up of interlacing patterns of words, expressions and themes (see the section on Versification, pp.81–6). The great buckle is covered with an interwoven snake design of geometric precision and symmetry that reflects an advanced culture and is reflected in the style of the imaginative poetry of the age.

A final point that might be made is the relationship between this English find and Sweden. Much of the jewelry is in Swedish style but was probably made in England, indeed East Anglia. The technique used is called cloisonné: gold-rimmed compartments are filled in with garnets or glass. The intricate snake-pattern on the sword-belt buckle is similarly English but of Swedish design. The sword and magnificent helmet are thought to have come from Sweden. The 'Swedish connection' with East

Anglia, therefore, confirms the Scandinavian link in *Beowulf*. The connection goes beyond artefacts to links in culture and indeed royal houses. Bede tells us that the first Anglo-Saxon kings of East Anglia were Wuffingas, a Swedish dynasty, and therefore it is certain that tales of early kings and heroes would have been common to Sweden and East Anglia, if not all of England. The hundred-year-old armour found at Sutton Hoo would go back to a time when the links with Sweden and paganism were strong and when the events in *Beowulf* took place.

Similarly, ship burials of the type found at Sutton Hoo were common only in Uppland in Sweden at this early date, although found all over Scandinavia in the later Viking period. The fact that no body was found in the ship might be explained by the mixture of Christian and pagan elements. Like Beowulf this Anglian king might have had two funerals: the first pagan and the second Christian.

Funeral customs

A closer look at the description of the funerals in *Beowulf* provides us with much cultural information. The poet dwells on the funerals and evidently attaches great significance to them. Beowulf himself receives two ceremonies: a definitely pagan cremation (as burning the body was forbidden by the church, which believed in resurrection of body and soul at Doomsday), and a burial in a grave mound that is ambiguously Christian or pagan. Mixed forms of burial were not uncommon in early Christian northern Europe when people had not totally renounced the safety of their traditional gods and wished to play safe when it came to such an important ceremony as a funeral. The third grave mound at Sutton Hoo contains a sixth-century cremation burial (that is, the body was burned and then given a grave burial), and there are many examples of partially burned skeletons presumably retrieved from the flames to be given a Christian burial. So Beowulf's double ceremony would have been common in sixth- and seventh-century England. In Sweden there are also traces of many great cremation ceremonies in which armour was also burned on the pyre.

The scene of horsemen riding round Beowulf's pyre reciting his great deeds is paralleled in a sixth-century description of the funeral of Attila the Hun. 'The finest horsemen in the whole Hunnish nation rode round and round the place where he [Atilla] was laid, as if in the circus games, while they proclaimed his deeds in a funeral dirge.' * Attila was also buried in an impressive grave mound which is laden with costly treasure and armour, but a more sinister note is added when those

* G.N. Garmonsway, J. Simpson and H.E. Davidson, *Beowulf and its Analogues*, Dent, London, 1968, p.340.

burying him are themselves slaughtered and buried with him. The grue-some details of the ritual murder of a slave-girl at her master's funeral are given in an eye-witness account by an Arab trader in c.922.* The cult of Woden demanded that the body should be cremated along with goods, and the ashes buried or thrown in the sea. There was also the belief that the higher the smoke rose, the loftier would be the position of the dead man in the next world. Consequently great care was taken in building fine pyres; and in *Beowulf* we hear the chieftains from far and wide would bring the wood for Beowulf's pyre which was high and broad (1.3157), and when lit became 'the biggest of funeral-fires. Black wood-smoke / arose from the blaze'.

It was also common in Christian times to bury possessions, even food, drink, armour, treasure, vessels, combs—indeed all that was necessary for the long journey into the unknown.

At the cremation funeral of Hnaef and Hildeburh's son (the Finn episode) we hear the graphic details of the fire eating up the bodies: 'There were melting heads / and bursting wounds, as the blood sprang out . . .' (ll.1120–2). Such vivid detail, many critics have stated, must come from someone well acquainted with cremation and it was there-fore probably known to the *Beowulf* poet. Hildeburh sings a dirge at the cremation, just as the Geatish woman does at Beowulf's. It was common for the widow to do this, and therefore many have assumed that Beowulf was married, perhaps to Hygd.

Beowulf's funeral, therefore, was probably what the poet would have expected for a great king and maybe he had witnessed such a cremation. One thing is sure—it is not Christian.

Scyld Shefing's funeral at the opening of the poem sounds extremely romantic, as if from a fairy tale. It reminds one of the mythical King Arthur's mystical departure from life on a splendid barge to a place from where he will return one day. Scyld arrived by boat laden with treasure as a child and a similar treasure is placed in his funeral ship as his body is pushed out to the sea 'to travel with him / on his far faring into the flood's sway'. The basic significance of a ship burial is obvious: the long journey from this world to the next. The attractive story of Scyld's funeral was considered imaginative and far-fetched until the Sutton Hoo discovery showed a similar treasure funeral ship. There are also accounts of the dead being placed on burning ships which are launched, another mixture of two traditions. Naturally we have only archaeological evidence of ship burials on land, and these are numer-ous enough. The church's fear of the evil-infested seas also forbade ship burials, as a body drowned at sea was considered eternally lost. So Scyld's funeral is also pagan. As ships were expensive items and could

* ibid., pp.341–2.

not be 'wasted' in such practices, there are many examples, especially in Sweden, of boat-shaped stone graves.

The Fight at Finnsburg

Many editions and translations of *Beowulf* append the 'Finnsburg Fragment' or 'The Fight at Finnsburg' to the text, because of its affinities with the Finn episode (ll.1063–1159). There is no medieval manuscript surviving of this forty-eight-line fragment of a poem, but in 1705 George Hickes, the eighteenth-century English scholar and editor of a *Thesaurus* of early texts, copied what he found on a single leaf (now lost) bound up with some sermons. The gist of the story we can piece together is as follows:

A Danish band of warriors under Hnaef is in the hall of the Frisian king, Finn. (We know from *Beowulf* that the Danish princess Hildeburh has married Finn to help create peace between two warring tribes.) A Danish sentinel in the night sees something flashing and Hnaef poetically replies that it is no fire, sunrise or dragon, but attackers. He rouses his men and tells them how to fight. The warriors arm, and two are stationed at each door. Guthere restrains Garulf from rushing out too early. The battle begins, shields split and swords spark; Garulf, son of Guthlaf, falls defending the door. Hnaef's sixty warriors fight brilliantly and the doors are still held five days later. The fragment ends with the suggestion that there are a number of casualties. The rest of the tale continues in the *Beowulf* episode when we hear of the deaths of Hnaef and Hildeburh's son. The story is succinctly told in a highly rhetorical style; there is some direct speech that heightens the tension and the sense of sudden danger and frantic action is well expressed. The technique of flashes of action reminds one of the ballad.

This fragment of a poem confirms critics' views that the Finn lay, like many other tales of heroic battles, was well known to the Anglo-Saxon audience. The *Beowulf* poet would take this for granted and *use* the story to highlight a specific theme or moral.

Part 4

Hints for study

Working with the texts

Beowulf was composed to be heard not read and this might apply to the modern poetic translations as well. If you cannot read Old English you could borrow one of the modern recordings of *Beowulf*. The effect of rhythm and sound patterns is lost when the work is read silently.

If you are working with a translation alone it would be wise to borrow a copy of Klaeber's edition and read the Introduction and Notes and use the Glossary. Other editions of the Old English text, for example, Wrenn's, are equally good, but Klaeber's glossary has detailed line references which will aid those working with a translation. His list of Proper Names is very detailed and helpful with etymological explanations. If you are going to build a theory on or support a point by a specific word or phrase, you should check with the original text or at least with a second translation in case the translation you use does not give a literal rendition. Here is a recent example of this problem: a student based his argument that there is serious criticism of the Danes in *Beowulf* on the phrase in Michael Alexander's translation '[Hrothgar's men] led a careless life' (l.99). Alexander's translation is accurate, but he uses 'careless' in the sense of 'free from care', whereas the student thought it meant 'thoughtless', 'without due care'. If the original had been consulted, the word *dreamum* would have been found, which Klaeber translates 'with joy' (a second translation gives 'joyously'). The student's argument about the Danes deserving Grendel could not be supported by this textual evidence. Free translations that capture the mood of *Beowulf* cannot be expected to give literal renditions of every word. If, for example, you are working on the theme of fate in *Beowulf*, you will find that Old English *wyrd* is translated in a number of different ways and, conversely, every occurrence of the word 'fate' in a translation need not necessarily render *wyrd*. It is safer to look up *wyrd* in Klaeber's glossary where every occurrence is noted with its line reference and then you can check with your translation.

Those who read Old English will also benefit from reading a good translation, such as Alexander's, as much of the meaning of the poem is conveyed by the mood and we can imagine that the poem would perhaps have been heard at one sitting. Few can read Old English so fluently as to read the entire work in an evening, so the overall effect, the accumulation of details that creates the tone of the poem, can be captured by reading a verse translation.

A reading of *Beowulf* will be simplified by a careful study, even memorisation, of the family trees (see p.4); this will avoid constant reference to them when you are concentrating on the text. It would also help to study the section on the Swedish Wars in these Notes (pp.68–9) before embarking on a discussion of the second part of *Beowulf*, as it is easy to become confused about chronology.

Answering an essay question

Quotations from *Beowulf* should be set out as follows.

If the quotation consists of only one or two lines, incorporate it within your sentence and write it like this: " <u>We synt Higelaces / beodge-natas; Beowulf is min nama</u> ", 'We are Hygelac's table companions; Beowulf is my name' (ll.342–3). (The division into lines of verse in the Old English text is indicated by oblique strokes /; it is not necessary to indicate these line divisions in your own translation.) The Old English is underlined and in *this* instance also enclosed in quotation marks because it is a speech by Beowulf; otherwise quotation marks should not be used for the Old English. (As shown, you can distinguish between such 'speech' quotations and the translations by putting the former in double and the latter in single quotation marks.) Here is another example, this time a short phrase: <u>sothfaestra dom,</u> 'the judgment of the righteous' (l.2820). If you are quoting one or two lines from a translation only, the same applies: use quotation marks and incorporate within your sentence.

If the Old English quotation is *more* than two lines, centre it on the page. Do not underline and do not use quotation marks (unless, as in the first example above, it is from a speech). The translation follows and can also be centred. If you are only using a translation, whether in prose or poetry, quotations from it of more than two lines should likewise be centred.

You should acknowledge in a note the source of the translation if it is not your own, such as 'All translations in this essay are from . . . ' and give full bibliographical information.

Try to give line references as often as possible, or a page reference if your translation has no line numbering. This will enable your readers to check textual evidence.

If you quote from a critical work, indent citations that are more than two lines and give your full bibliographical reference in a note, not in your text. Add a list of works you have consulted at the conclusion of your essay with bibliographical information. See Part 5, 'Suggestions for further reading' in these Notes for examples.

It is important to quote or paraphrase the text with line references in order to support your argument, but do not simply string together a number of relevant quotations without any explanation or discussion. You cannot expect the reader to come to the same conclusion as you without commentary. Quotations back up your points but should not be a substitute for argument. There is a golden mean between too many and too few quotations.

Never overestimate the time it takes to formulate and present your essay, whether at home or in an examination situation. Part of the exercise is to see how you argue and present the material, and whether you are clear and logical in your thinking. Many say that the accumulation of information, the 'research' part of essay writing, is only half the battle. Write a clear introduction in which you outline the scope and aim of your essay as well as the critical methods to be used. You may like to add necessary background material here. The central part of your essay will be a well-documented and logically prepared argument in which you present your material; then you should add a succinct conclusion in which you draw together the threads of the argument and finally restate your major point. Endnotes and bibliography conclude the work.

Old English poetry

Versification

The Old English verse line is based on stress, not the number of syllables in a line. Each verse line is divided into two half-lines by a central pause or caesura; in modern editions this break is clearly marked by space in the middle of a line:

> gyddum geomore | | thaette Grendel wan
> in grievous songs | | how Grendel warred

Each half-line has two stressed syllables (/) and two or more unstressed syllables (×):

> / ×   / × ×   × × / × /
> gyddum geomore | | thaette Grendel wan
> × / × /   ×   / × /
> in grievous songs | | how Grendel warred

The two half-lines, therefore, balance each other with two stresses each.

Old English words, as in other Germanic languages, have a stress on the *first* syllable (unless there is a prefix like *be-*, *ge-*, etc.). It is only natural therefore that rhyme in poetry falls on the first syllables of the word: this front-rhyme is called alliteration; for example, 'grievous' and 'Grendel' alliterate. Alliteration occurs when the words begin with the same consonant or consonant cluster, such as *sp*, *st*, *sc*, or with a vowel, as all vowels alliterate with each other.

In the Old English verse line, usually three of the four stressed syllables alliterate; the first stressed syllable of the second half-line alliterates with at least one, often both, of the stressed syllables of the first half-line. For example:

```
  /         /              /          /
gyddum geomore        thaette Grendel wan
or :
  /          /             /          /
Beowulf waes  breme    blaed wide sprang
(Beowulf was famous    his fame sprang afar)
```

The second stressed syllable of the second half-line rarely alliterates. This 'sound echo' of alliteration also gives a balance and a unity to the poetic line and emphasises the important words. Much variation can occur within this pattern, for example in the number of unstressed syllables and in the position of the stressed syllables. It is also possible to have rare hypermetric lines, for example, ll.1163−8 and 1705−7, with more than two stresses per half-line.

Vocabulary

The Old English poet enjoyed using poetic diction, often old-fashioned words: for example, *mece* for sword, *hleo* (shelter), *hild* (battle), *holm* (sea). A ship would be called *ceol*, literally 'keel' and a shield *lind*, literally 'linden-wood'. This is called metonymy, when the part of an object stands for the whole.

One step further from literal description is the popular *kenning* : a kenning is a condensed simile, usually in the form of a compound word. For example, a sail is a 'sea-garment' (*mere-hraegl*, l.1905); the sea itself is called 'the swan's riding place' (*swan-rad*, l.200); the sun is 'the candle of the heavens' (*rodores candel*, l.1572); a sword is 'the leavings of the hammer' (*homera laf*, l.2829).

A large number of compound words are found in Old English verse. Many of these are only found in poetry and many are originally coined by the *Beowulf* poet. Each part of the compound would be known but the originality lay in placing them together; for example, *lig-yth*, 'fire-flame', l.2672; *fifel-cyn*, 'race of monsters', l.104; *fen-hlith*, 'fen-slope', l.820; *ferhth-genithla*, 'deadly foe', l.2881; *feorh-last*, 'life-trace', l.846.

Old English vocabulary gathers clusters of meanings as it is repeatedly heard in different contexts. Words like *wyrd*, 'fate', 'Providence', or *dom*, 'glory', 'reputation', have dozens of associations, pagan and Christian alike. There is no attempt to be scientifically precise and this blurring of associations reflects the mentality of a people who could accept the old, pagan words and temples as suitable for the new religion. The image of new wine into old bottles is often used and this new wine is given an extra flavour because of it.

Style

The love of newly coined words and compounds is akin to the devices of circumlocution, for example, when the poet does not state that Scyld defeated enemies but 'took mead-benches' (*meodosetla ofteah*, l.5); and euphemism, for example, 'journey elsewhere' (*ellorsith*, l.2451) for death. Superlatives also abound in *Beowulf*, as in *husa selest*, 'the best of houses' (ll.146, 285, 935).

Possibly the most common poetic device is *variation*: a word or expression is repeated, not identically, and each repetition adds a new attribute or quality to the concept. Hrothgar, for example, is called by Beowulf 'son of Healfdene', 'guardian of the people', 'glorious hero', 'Shepherd of the Danes', and each title adds another quality to Hrothgar. Grendel is called 'the walker in the night', 'the demon', 'the spoiler', 'monster', 'this warlike creature', 'the foe', 'the ravager', 'terrible solitary one', 'the rough marauder', 'God's enemy', 'the damned one', 'wanderer in the border regions' and much more. In this way, although we have no long description of the monster, each epithet adds to our understanding of Grendel. A complex and nuanced picture of the *nature* of this monster gradually emerges concerning his strength, abode, spiritual state, intentions, time of attacks, and so on. Before his third fight Beowulf is called within a few lines 'leader', 'warrior king', 'champion of fighting men', 'prince of rings', and thus his strength, leadership, nobility and generosity are elicited. We could also analyse the epithets for God and find that one particular attribute is pointed out each time.

In the same way this technique of variation functions with larger units than words; for example, Beowulf's successes are repeated two or three times. But at no point is this mere repetition; with each retelling new information is added; for example, on Beowulf's return to Geatland he adds the information about Grendel's pouch and the story of Freawaru. The technique is basically that of oral storytelling when an episode is repeated but with one or more significant changes.

Interlacing technique

Connected with the theme of variation are the interlacing methods of
the poet. John Leyerle's research has clearly demonstrated the parallel
between interlace designs in Anglo-Saxon jewelry, weapons and illustrated manuscripts and the poet's technique. He quotes ll.2354−9 of
Beowulf as an example of 'interwoven variation':

> That was not the least
> of hand-to-hand encounters where Hygelac was killed,
> when the King of the Geats in the rush of the battle
> the beloved friend of the people, in Frisia,
> the son of Hrethel died bloodily,
> struck down with the sword.

The simple statement made is that Hygelac was killed in battle with the
Frisians. The terms for Hygelac are underlined, terms for 'was killed'
are dotted and the location is marked with a broken line. These three
statements are intricately woven together to create a complex, poetic
picture of the event.*

Formulas

The Old English poets talk about their 'word hoard'; they would have,
at least in the oral tradition, a stock of verse formulas, expressions,
often half-lines, which would suit the particular occasion. Sometimes it
would be convenient to find a ready alliteration, such as *gold on
grunde* (l.2765), 'gold on the ground'. The formula could be longer
than a half-line and, with suitable variation, express the recurrent
battle scene with beasts of battle, swords clashing, shields breaking,
and so on.

Such a definition of stock formulas makes the oral poet's function
appear dull and unimaginative. But this is far from the truth; because
of the expected repetition of a phrase any slight change would be all the
more significant. We hear, for example, of the legendary Scyld: *thaet
waes god cyning*, 'that was a good king' (l.11). We know he is an exemplary, model king, so when this phrase is used to describe Hrothgar
(l.863) and Beowulf (l.2390) we compare them, and by this brief asso-
ciation the two later kings are raised to the mythical heights of the
perfect king Scyld. Perhaps it is also significant that Hygelac is not
granted this stock phrase. Variation of the adjectives from *god* to

* John Leyerle, 'The Interlace Structure of *Beowulf*', *University of Toronto Quarterly*,
1967, pp.1−17.

grimme, 'evil', conveys much more than face value, as we are invited to *contrast* with these exemplary monarchs.

You should remember that Old English poetry was composed to be recited aloud, possibly accompanied by a lute, such as that found in the Sutton Hoo treasure: 'Then string and song sounded together . . . the lute was taken up and tales recited' (ll.1063 and 1065). The *scop* or poet was a professional and an honoured member of the court, for it was he who not only entertained but kept the treasure-house of legends and the tribe's history alive, and played the vital role of preserving the memory, reputation and thence afterlife of dead heroes. There are many parallels between the influence and importance of a king's treasure and the store of verse his *scop* kept in circulation, and it is not surprising that the Sutton Hoo treasure contained a lute as well as gold and armour. The term 'word-hoard' is frequently applied to Old English verse and the term *scop* implies a creator, a moulder of these words. His methods are described in *Beowulf*, ll.867−74:

> Or a fellow of the king's,
> whose head was a storehouse of the storied verse,
> whose tongue gave gold to the language
> of the treasured repertory, wrought a new lay
> made in the measure. The man struck up,
> found the phrase, framed rightly
> the deed of Beowulf, drove the tale,
> rang word-changes.

We learn from this that the 'scop' created a new heroic lay with little preparation; he takes from his golden word-hoard the right phrase, remoulds certain phrases or formulas, 'rings word-changes' (*wordum wrixlan*, l.874) and thereby moulds his new song. Perhaps this last phrase refers to the technique of variation, mentioned above, when the slight variation draws the listener's attention to a new aspect.

In your studies you will probably meet the major discussion in Old English scholarship about the nature of the composition of the early poetry. Was *Beowulf* first written down using well-known, earlier oral techniques, or did it snowball from a small oral poem to a bigger one that someone eventually put on vellum, or is the answer somewhere between the two theories? Was there one single *Beowulf* poet? Old English scholars like Magoun have built on the important thesis of Parry on the composition of oral poetry, supported by analyses of modern Yugoslavian oral poets' techniques. Formulaic phrases and entire scenes could be reworked to create long, oral tales, improvising new stories on traditional formulas. It is highly probable that early Germanic poets used the same techniques.

The key to Old English poetic style is 'freedom within form'. The versification, stock epithets, the rhetoric of wars, the repetition of the exploits of heroes like Sigemund would not have been original, yet the poet had great freedom within these set and indeed expected patterns to create original, alive and fresh verse. The beauty of the language in *Beowulf*, the repetition and variations, the rhythm, are all part of the meaning. We see the significance of poetry in Anglo-Saxon society in this poem. The silence of the harp and the poet is a euphemism for the breakdown of society, for example, when Grendel rules Heorot. The songs reappear after the re-establishment of an ordered society and it is not surprising that the description of the creation of Heorot is immediately followed by the Song of the World's Creation. When Wiglaf predicts the exile and total isolation of the cowardly Geats he expresses their predicament in terms of the cessation of harp and melody.

Suggested questions

1. Discuss the unity of *Beowulf*.
2. Select a few of the episodes or 'digressions' and discuss their function.
3. To what extent is *Beowulf* a Christian poem?
4. Is *Beowulf* a tragedy?
5. Discuss the significance of Hrothgar's 'sermon'.
6. What part does Weird or Fate play in the poem?
7. What does *Beowulf* tell us about early Germanic society and culture?
8. Discuss the significance of treasure and gold-giving in *Beowulf*.
9. Discuss the concepts of praise and reputation (*lof* and *dom*) in *Beowulf*.
10. What aspects of the poem most appeal to you?
11. Make your own poetic rendition of a section of *Beowulf*.

Guidelines to answers

1. Discuss the unity of *Beowulf*.

(*a*) You could begin by showing the unity and simplicity of the basic plot: a Geatish prince overcomes two monsters in Denmark in his early days and kills, but is slain by, a dragon in his old age.

(*b*) The character of Beowulf himself creates a strong unifying effect all through the poem.

(*c*) You could show how the poem is divided into two major geographic areas, Denmark and Geatland and the courts of Hrothgar and Hygelac. There are many links between these two sections: a young prince and an older king (Beowulf and Hrothgar in the first section and Wiglaf and King Beowulf in the second); monsters and a dragon; survival, success, death, and so on.

(*d*) There are also many strong contrasts that create unity by balancing the two sections: youth and age, hope and despair, success and failure; heroism and cowardliness, joy and sorrow, order and disorder, evil and good, life and death. Some critics talk about the entire poem as a balance of opposites.

(*e*) You could compare and contrast the life and atmosphere in the halls of Hrothgar, Hygelac and Beowulf, the two queens, Wealhtheow and Hygd, the banquets, the funerals, the armouring scenes.

(*f*) There are many other uniting themes that run through the work—treasure and gold, loyalty and *comitatus* ideals, praise and reputation, and fate.

(*g*) You might discuss the cyclical nature of the events. The poem begins and ends with the funerals of great kings and throughout the poem we see men raised to power, being successful, plunging into despair because of reversed fortune (the theme of sorrow after joy) and finally returning to a joyful state.

(*h*) You will have to tackle the criticism of lack of unity caused by the so-called 'digressions', the episodes of Finn and Ingeld and the shorter accounts of Heremod and Sigemund, as well as the gnomic or moralising sections that are added. The question of the digressions will be dealt with in the next answer below, but you should stress the fact that *Beowulf* is not a linear narrative, and point to the chronological complexities of the Swedish Wars. The poet rarely creates suspense, but invariably tells us the outcome long before the fight. The digressions help to create the mood and moral message that the poet hopes to convey. Beowulf's or Hygd's character is not described directly, but by comparison with Heremod and Offa's cruel queen, respectively.

(*i*) The key to the problem of unity, apart from the narrative framework and unifying themes mentioned above, is in the tone, mood and message conveyed. For this reason the directly moralising speeches, the 'sermon' by Hrothgar and the longer 'digressions' are added.

(*j*) Naturally, it is not necessary to search all the time for unifying themes. Michael Alexander in the Introduction (pp.39–41) to his translation suggests differences in structure between the two halves of the poem that could point to separate authorship. Here you could mention the methods of possible oral composition of Old English verse. (See the section on Old English poetry in these Notes, pp.81–6.)

2. Select a few of the episodes or 'digressions' and discuss their function.

(a) The 'digressions' in *Beowulf* range from minor passages of moralising, such as ll.20–25 (often called gnomic passages as they contain some wise saying or maxim) to much larger sections. You could mention the narrator's own comments that some might call intruding, such as ll.82–5, when the future tragedy of the Danes is predicted. Other minor interpolations are the accounts of the Brising necklace, the history of the giant-sword Beowulf found in Grendel's cave and the history of the race that hid the treasure which the dragon later guarded. Longer episodes include the Sigemund section, in which Beowulf is compared with the legendary dragon-slayer, the Breca swimming match, the story of Heremod and the account of Offa's cruel queen. Finally, there are the major 'digressions' such as the tales of Finn and of Ingeld, the sermon by Hrothgar and the Swedish Wars which are recounted in a series of flashbacks at the conclusion of the poem.

(b) Having identified the passages which can be said to detract from the narrative it would be best to select a few, as stated in the question, and look at them closely in context. As suggested above, the key to the problem is to view the poem not as a flowing narrative with 'digressions' but as a static work that creates a mood and argument by repeating certain themes. In this way the incidents mentioned above are seen no longer as digressions but as an integral part of this aim. Just as the poet uses the technique of variation (see p.83), he also varies themes and maxims by presenting them in different guises. We have seen above how he describes characters by comparing and contrasting them. We are expected to know already about Sigemund, and the poet has no intention of retelling that incident. Its function is to elevate Beowulf to the ranks of the great, legendary heroes.

(c) A minor but good example to take might be the Brising necklace which is compared with the gift Wealhtheow presens to Beowulf. The significance of this passage is discussed on pp.72–3 above, but the crucial point is that the Brising necklace is steeped in tales of deceit and treachery and that Wealhtheow's gift will later be found on Hygelac when his foolhardy expedition fails and the necklace passes into enemy hands. The *context* of this incident is vital. It adds a note of treachery and failure at a point when Wealhtheow hopes to buy future peace in Denmark and secure her sons' succession by giving Beowulf treasure. We have had other suggestions of future disaster, but this hint is even more subtle and functions by creating a *mood* of treachery without direct allusion.

(d) Having demonstrated the poet's technique and use of these episodes, it would then be timely for you to discuss one of the major stories. You could take the episode of the Swedish Wars and show how the history of

Dano-Swedish hostility prepares us for a crisis and calamity after Beowulf's death, without definite proof. Given the Germanic spirit of vengeance and the background of war, major conflict becomes inevitable.

(e) The tales of Finn and Ingeld come at times of rejoicing and success, and basically reinforce the message of 'woe after joy', the fleeting nature of peace and happiness in such a society and the constant presence of reprisals and revenge. A comparison of these two incidents would help to demonstrate the poet's aims. Both deal with the need for revenge by thanes; both stress the failure of inter-tribal marriage to create peace—in fact it is more likely to cause renewed warfare (see Beowulf's personal comments in ll.2026−31). Both deal with the plight of women as pawns in the war-game, and the insoluble dilemma of mixed loyalties caused by inter-marriage. Finally, both incidents prepare us for future disaster; not only the burning of Heorot and renewed feuding, but also this note of hopelessness, as far as peace and joy are concerned, which forebodes imminent disaster in the poem itself. Just as Hrothgar in his sermon, which again occurs at a moment of celebration, warns Beowulf that his success cannot continue, so also the inclusion of these episodes reinforces the warning. The Finn episode looks back at past disaster, the Ingeld story predicts future conflict stemming from good intentions, so that the mood of rejoicing at success that precedes both incidents is dampened when we realise the continual swing from joy to sorrow and back again. In this way the so-called 'digressions' are of major importance in creating the tone and thus forming the meaning of the poem.

(f) An episode such as the story of Breca and the swimming match can easily be shown to be a literary device to demonstrate Beowulf's prowess. He cannot in all humility enter Hrothgar's court and sing his own praises, so it is necessary for Unferth to accuse Beowulf of pride and of being unable to carry out his heroic boasts. The incident shows Beowulf as a great hero having supernatural strength, and as being an extraordinarily good swimmer. These qualities prepare us for his later feats of valour. In addition we are told that he cleansed the seas of evil forces and made seafaring less dangerous. This creates a link with the underwater battle later and with Beowulf's barrow as a beacon for sailors.

---

3. To what extent is *Beowulf* a Christian poem?

(a) You could point out that sixth-century Scandinavians could not have been Christian, and Christianity first came to England at the close of that century. The *Beowulf* poet is undoubtedly Christian and a mood of spiritual concern permeates the poem. The key to the problem lies in the ease with which heroic (or pagan) and Christian ideas and ideals were interchanged; or rather the felicitous adaptation by Christian missionaries of existing concepts and their ability to 'baptise' and adopt Germanic tenets. Read the sections on Weird and Fate, praise and glory, funeral customs and Hrothgar's sermon in Part 3 of these Notes to see how the Christian Anglo-Saxon made use of the territory common to both traditions.

(b) Beowulf's cremation is undoubtedly pagan, possibly connected with the Germanic cult of Woden, but Beowulf is never called 'heathen', as are Grendel and his mother; he inhabits the misty no-man's-land between pagan and Christian traditions. Perhaps the poet cannot call him heathen without detracting from his reputation, yet knows Beowulf is not Christian.

(c) The problem of pinning Beowulf down to one or the other creed does not aid our understanding of the poem, any more than worrying about the question of Troilus's Christianity in Chaucer's *Troilus and Criseyde* (c.1380). Beowulf is never criticised for not being Christian; he mentions God's help and acknowledges his dependence on Him, and the qualities the poet ascribes to Beowulf on his death are the Christian ones of meekness, gentleness and kindness, as well as the primal heroic virtue of being 'most eager for fame'.

(d) The biblical allusions in the poem are nearly all from the Old Testament—the Creation of the World, Cain, the Flood, but there is no mention of Christ, of angels, saints, heaven or any New Testament event. The virtues of the New Testament, roughly summed up as loving and caring, are present in Beowulf's character, whereas the Old Testament call for revenge and 'an eye for an eye' seems to dominate all other characters.

(e) You could discuss the much-debated section, ll.170−88, in which the Danes indulge in the worship of heathen gods. The poet implies that the Christian God was unknown to them, and it appears as if this is not a reference to a temporary backslide into heathen practices at a moment of crisis. Such reversions to paganism were well known in England, as Bede bears witness in his *Ecclesiastical History*. The poet deliberately states that the Danes neither knew nor had heard of God. Hrothgar, however, frequently calls on God and gives thanks to Him. An easy solution would be to say that this passage was interpolated by a later, Christian scribe. But an answer may be found in the poet's conscious artistry: he wishes to create a mood of depression at the lowest point of Danish despair during Grendel's attacks. Nothing can help them and their gods are useless; their affliction is *nihtbealwa maest*, 'worst of nightmares' (l.193), too cruel, too harsh and too long, we hear. Clause after clause in this passage builds up a mood of fear, terror and total despair and at this nadir of Danish history the poet changes style abruptly, launching into highly rhetorical poetry that describes the optimism surrounding Beowulf's first appearance. The passage creates a mood and a contrast and is not intended as a serious statement of theology.

(*f*) You could refer to the natural mixture of Christian and pagan items in the Sutton Hoo burial ship or in many Anglo-Saxon artefacts, such as the Frank's Casket with its carvings of the story of the Adoration of the Magi and Weland the Smith side by side. Typical of this mingling of two cultures is the description of the dragon's curse in *Beowulf*; a pagan spell is clothed in a Christian formula—a curse is put on the treasure and the punishment is Christian damnation at Doomsday.

(*g*) Deliberate ambiguity is a key word when discussing this problem. Beowulf's soul, we hear, seeks *sothfaestra dom*, 'the glory of the righteous', whatever that is. There is no specific reference to either pagan or Christian afterlife. It is as if the poet deliberately does not take sides. *Whatever* code Beowulf embraced he excelled and was its paragon, and he received whatever reward is given to such people. There are times when Beowulf with his loyal followers appears a saviour-figure and critics have pointed to many allusions that remind one of Christ. It would limit the poem to read it as a Christian allegory, but the hints are there and they, like the comparison with the heroic Sigemund, serve to enhance Beowulf's reputation without restricting him. Beowulf lives in a 'religious vacuum' which shows both that the poet admires and is attracted to heroic ideals and that as a Christian he is unable to grant Beowulf Christian salvation. He can pass sentence of eternal damnation on the monsters and the devil-worshippers, but he pays Beowulf the compliment of being silent about the state of his soul.

(*h*) Do not use the example of blood-revenge as evidence for paganism, as the early church supported or at least did not frown on revenge. We can see the deep-rooted nature of this well into modern times and exemplified in Shakespeare's *Hamlet* or Kyd's *The Spanish Tragedy*. The Old Testament 'an eye for an eye' and the God of Vengeance provided textual evidence enough to permit the continuation of this code.

(*i*) The most significant clue to the Christianity of *Beowulf* is to be found in the *tone* of the poem. The poet places much emphasis on peace, whereas we saw that Tacitus claimed peace was unwise, as it did not refill the coffers of the 'gold-giver' and made the warriors restless. A strong and high-born class of society that is idle, especially when trained in warfare, is a danger. Klaeber lists a number of Christian 'hints', such as Beowulf's gratitude to God and the sympathetic treatment of Scyld and Grendel, and he calls Beowulf 'somewhat tame, sentimental, and fond of talking' (p.1). The ethos of the poem is that of established Anglo-Saxon Christianity, and the poet's knowledge of the Bible and the offices of the day supports this theory. He simply plays down *direct* Christian allusions and omits New Testament references altogether in his attempt to recapture the mood of early Germanic life. Most of the values and morals are identical and the poet follows the enlightened missionaries' methods of stressing that area of common thought.

4. Is *Beowulf* a tragedy?

(*a*) You should define tragedy to begin with, remembering that in the Middle Ages it need not only refer to drama. The medieval view of tragedy was simply the reversal of the fortunes, hence the fall, of a great man. Geoffrey Chaucer's (*c*.1343–*c*.1400) Monk in *The Canterbury Tales* (*c*.1387–1400) gives a succinct definition, as well as examples:

> Tragedie is to seyn [say] a certeyn storie, . . .
> Of hym that stood in greet prosperitee,
> And is yfallen out of heigh degree [high position]
> Into myserie, and endeth wrecchedly.
> *The Prologue of the Monk's Tale*, ll.1973–7.

You might also like to speculate about other genres that *Beowulf* might belong to, for example the epic. Michael Alexander in the Introduction to his translation deals with *Beowulf*'s epic qualities at length.

(*b*) You might like to concentrate on the conclusion of the poem to see the extent of Beowulf's 'wrecched end'. From a Geatish viewpoint his death is tragic. Chaos and possible annihilation will ensue; all that Beowulf has created over fifty years will collapse and the feuds and monsters will take over. As there is no Christian consolation and no afterlife other than fame mentioned, some might claim that Beowulf is a tragic figure.

(*c*) You could point to the tragic events and interludes throughout the poem that create the overall mood of despair. A prime example is the tragedy of Hrethel, the old king forced into an impossible situation by the laws of the Germanic code. One son has killed another by accident and one cannot take vengeance on a kinsman, yet it is a great shame to leave a dead son unavenged. Hrethel simply dies of a broken heart, as social rules have made life insufferable. The predicament of Hildeburh in the Finn episode is also tragic: she loses brother, son and then husband through no fault of her own. Freawaru in the Ingeld episode is equally the innocent and tragic victim of the code of vengeance.

(*d*) Tragic anticipation frequently occurs and this helps to create a tragic tone. The poet will say 'it was not yet the time for the hall to burn or for uncle and nephew to fight'. All times of joy and celebration are overshadowed by hints of imminent tragedy and a melancholic atmosphere permeates the tale. By blurring the distinction between good and bad, tragic situations arise. The Swedish king Ongentheow is described in warm terms, as is his Geatish opponent; the old king fights to retrieve his aged wife, the young Eofor is Hygelac's loyal thane and is executing his rightful and expected role. The fault, if any, lies with the system which frequently places its adherents in impossible situations, conflicting loyalties and senseless battles.

(e) Having pointed out tragic elements and the pervasive mood of tragedy, you could then counter your argument by showing how the hero, Beowulf, cannot really be called tragic. He achieves all he set out to do, he kills all monsters and dragons, saves Denmark, rules successfully for fifty years of peace and is an exemplary king. He achieves immortality through fame, is perfect in all things and dies with no regrets. No better death could be imagined for such a hero. Fifty years of peace was exceptional in those days and the Geats should be thankful. You could briefly compare the conclusions of *Beowulf* and another Danish tragedy, *Hamlet*. Both end with a ray of hope in the figures of Wiglaf and Fortinbras who will restore order.

(f) You might look at the geographic locations—the beauty of Heorot and the gloomy, terrifying home of the monsters. Such a difference reflects the moods of joy and tragedy that the poet wishes to create.

(g) Finally, you might query the usefulness of placing this work in any genre; it has elements of tragedy, epic, lay and saga. The attraction of the poem lies in the fact that the poet is able to capture the mixture of tragedy and joy, failure and success, fear and hope that makes up life. His major theme, as clearly seen in Hrothgar's sermon, is that life is like a wheel: tragedy must follow success and vice versa. One also perceives, through the poet's attraction to the heroic code, a sense of its futility: it embodies major flaws, for example in its strict code of vengeance, which place man in situations of tragically conflicting loyalties.

Part 5

Suggestions for further reading

The Old English text

KLAEBER, F. (ED.): *Beowulf and the Fight at Finnsburg*, D.C. Heath, Boston, 3rd edn with Supplements, 1950. This is the edition used for these Notes. Readers using a translation will also benefit from Klaeber's excellent Introduction, extensive notes and bibliography.

WRENN, C.L. (ED.): *Beowulf with the Finnesburg Fragment*, Harrap, London; St. Martin's Press, New York, 3rd edn, revised by W.F. Bolton, 1973. Also contains an excellent Introduction and Commentary.

Translations

Beowulf, a Verse Translation by Michael Alexander, Penguin Books, Harmondsworth, 1973. This is the translation used for these Notes. Alexander captures the mood and tone of the original in this excellent poetic rendition.

Beowulf and the Finnesburg Fragment, translated by J.R. Clark Hall, revised by C.L. Wrenn, George Allen & Unwin, London, 1950. This provides a more literal, prose translation and contains an introductory essay on Old English versification by J.R.R. Tolkien.

Background works

BLAIR, PETER HUNTER: *Introduction to Anglo-Saxon England*, Cambridge University Press, Cambridge, 1956.

CHAMBERS, R.W.: *Beowulf: An Introduction*, with Supplement by C.L. Wrenn, Cambridge University Press, Cambridge, 3rd edn, 1959.

GARMONSWAY, G.N., SIMPSON, J. and DAVIDSON, H.E.: *Beowulf and its Analogues*, Dent, London, 2nd edn, 1980. Contains a prose translation of the text, translations of relevant background material and a section on archaeology.

WHITELOCK, DOROTHY: *The Beginnings of English Society*, Penguin Books, Harmondsworth, 1952.

WILSON, DAVID M.: *The Anglo-Saxons*, Penguin Books, Harmondsworth, 1971. Anglo-Saxon culture, art and archaeology.

Studies on the text

FRY, DONALD K. (ED.): *The Beowulf Poet: A Collection of Critical Essays*, Twentieth Century Views, Prentice-Hall, Englewood Cliffs, N.J., 1968.

IRVING, EDWARD B., Jr.: *A Reading of Beowulf*, Yale University Press, New Haven, Conn., 1968.

NICHOLSON, L.E. (ED.): *An Anthology of Beowulf Criticism*, University of Notre Dame Press, Notre Dame, Ind., 1963. Eighteen essays including the important British Academy lecture by J.R.R. Tolkien, 'Beowulf: the monsters and the critics', pp.51–103.

WHITELOCK, DOROTHY: *The Audience of Beowulf*, Clarendon Press, Oxford, 1951.

SHIPPEY, T.A.: *Beowulf*. Studies in English Literature, no. 70, Edward Arnold, London, 1978.

SISAM, KENNETH: *The Structure of Beowulf*, Clarendon Press, Oxford, 1965.

Learning Old English

Readers of *Beowulf* in translation might be inspired by this poem to learn more about other Old English texts and the Old English language.

BARNEY, S.A.: *Word-hoard: An Introduction to Old English Vocabulary*, Yale University Press, New Haven, Conn., 1977.

BRADLEY, S.A.J.: *Anglo-Saxon Poetry*, Dent, London, 1982. Excellent introductions to and prose translations of practically all Old English poetry.

GREENFIELD, S.B.: *A Critical History of Old English Literature*, New York University Press, New York, 1965.

MOORE, S. and KNOTT, T.A.: *The Elements of Old English Elementary Grammar, Reference Grammar and Reading Selections*, University of Michigan Press, Ann Arbor, Mich., rev. edn, 1976.

QUIRK, R. and WRENN, C.L.: *An Old English Grammar*, Methuen, London, 2nd edn, 1963.

SWEET, H.: *The Student's Dictionary of Anglo-Saxon*, Oxford University Press, Oxford, 1897, reissued 1967.

The author of these notes

GRAHAM D. CAIE is senior lecturer in the English Department of the University of Copenhagen where he teaches medieval English studies. His publications include *The Judgment Day Theme in Old English Poetry* and a number of articles on Old English and Chaucer studies, as well as Chaucer's *The Merchant's Tale* in the York Notes series.